The Moons
of Our
Solar System

By the Same Author

Colonies in Orbit
Eavesdropping on Space
Harnessing the Sun
Thirty-Two Moons
The Tiny Planets
Galaxies, Islands in Space

*A stunning view of Jupiter taken by Voyager 1 when the space
probe was 17.5 million miles from the giant planet. The Great
Red Spot and three of Jupiter's four largest moons are visible.
Io is seen against Jupiter's disk, Europa is to the right, and Callisto
is barely visible at the bottom left.*

The Moons of Our Solar System

Newly Revised Edition

David C. Knight

Illustrated with diagrams by Ellen Cullen
and photographs

William Morrow and Company/New York/1980

Library of Congress Cataloging in Publication Data

Knight, David C
  The moons of our solar system.

  Previous ed. published in 1974 under title: Thirty-two moons.
  Summary: Discusses the possible origins, composition, and characteristics of the natural satellites in the solar system. Incorporates data from the Voyager and Pioneer flights.
  1. Satellites—Juvenile literature. [1. Satellites.   2. Solar system]
I. Cullen, Ellen.   II. Title.
QB401.K58   1980   523.9'8   80-369
ISBN 0-688-22230-7
ISBN 0-688-32230-1 lib. bdg.

Printed in the United States of America.
1   2   3   4   5   6   7   8   9   10

Picture credits:

Lick Observatory, University of California, page 118
Yerkes Observatory, University of Chicago, pages 95
  (photographed by E. C. Slipher), 112 (photographed by G. P. Kuiper)
All other photographs courtesy of NASA

The author wishes to express his thanks and appreciation to Dr. Lloyd Motz, of Columbia University, for checking his manuscript.

Contents

The Moons
of Our Solar System

More than a decade has passed since earthmen landed on the natural satellite of their own planet. In the decades ahead—sometime in the twenty-first century—they will almost certainly visit the natural satellites of other planets in the solar system.

In the case of four—Jupiter, Saturn, Uranus, and Neptune —earthmen will probably get no closer to them than their satellites. Landing on these giant planets themselves, with their intensely cold outer temperatures and forbidding, gaseous atmospheres, would be next to impossible.

Earthmen, however, will be able to study the outer planets in another way. Jupiter has fourteen known satellites and possibly more; Saturn has twelve known ones; Uranus has five; Neptune has two. From one or more of these natural satellites, perpetually orbiting their primaries, or parent bodies, men will be able to observe these outer worlds of the sun's family closely.

Astronomers define a natural satellite as a celestial body that revolves around one of the planets of the solar system. The moon is Earth's natural satellite. By analogy, the natural

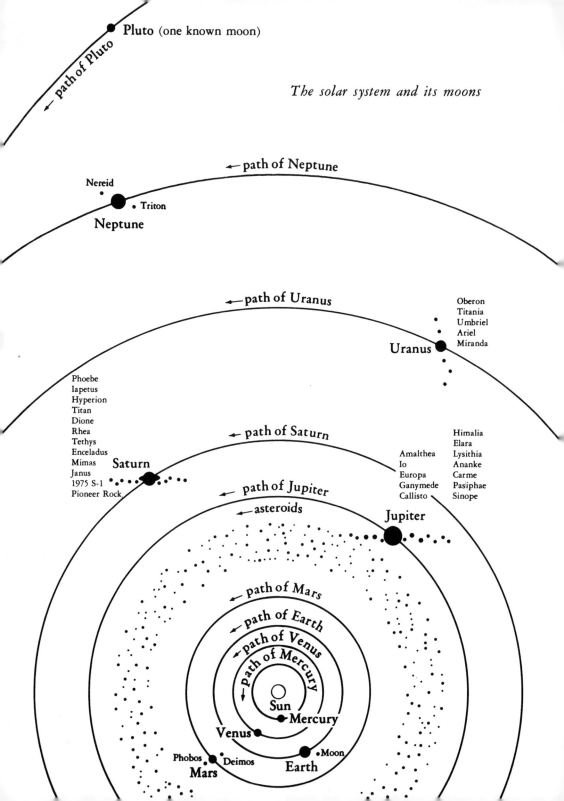

Pluto (one known moon)

← path of Pluto

The solar system and its moons

← path of Neptune

Nereid

Neptune • Triton

← path of Uranus

Oberon
Titania
Umbriel
Ariel
Miranda

Uranus

Phoebe
Iapetus
Hyperion
Titan
Dione
Rhea
Tethys
Enceladus
Mimas
Janus
1975 S-1
Pioneer Rock

← path of Saturn

Saturn

Himalia
Elara
Lysithia
Ananke
Carme
Pasiphae
Sinope

Amalthea
Io
Europa
Ganymede
Callisto

← path of Jupiter

Jupiter

← asteroids

← path of Mars
← path of Earth
← path of Venus
← path of Mercury

Sun

Mercury

Venus

Phobos • Deimos
Mars

• Moon
Earth

satellites of other planets are often called "moons" in popular scientific literature, although the term *natural satellite* is preferred by astronomers.

Besides Earth and the four giant planets, two others possess a satellite system. One is Mars, which has two small moons. The other is Pluto; its one moon was just discovered in 1978, and next to nothing is known about it. The remaining planets—Mercury and Venus—have no known natural satellites.

Some of these moons of our solar system are very small, no more than 10 miles or so in diameter. But six are as large or larger than our own moon, which has a diameter of 2,160 miles. Like Earth's moon, most of the others are probably barren, bleak worlds. Many probably lack atmospheres of any significance. They are also bitterly cold, for at such vast distances from the sun they receive very little light and heat.

Technically there are many more natural satellites than these in the solar system. The rings of Saturn, for example, consist of countless millions of tiny particles—most thought to be ice-coated bits of rock. Each is really a minuscule satellite of this giant planet. Nor are scientists certain that Pluto, discovered as late as 1930, is the last planet in the solar system. If it is not, still more distant planets that possess moons may be discovered.

How did these moons of our solar system originate? Why

do so some planets have several? Why do some have none? At present scientists cannot answer these questions because they are not in agreement about how the solar system itself originated.

In the last 200 years of scientific thought, there have been approximately half a dozen serious theories proposed to explain the origin of the solar system. Today scientists tend to favor two of them, or variations of them, and they may offer a clue as to how the moons themselves might have originated.

One modern hypothesis of the origin of the solar system was proposed by the American astronomer Gerard P. Kuiper. He assumed there was originally a disk-shaped nebula (a gaseous cloud) of tremendous extent, with the protosun (the sun-to-be) at its center. The overall composition of the nebula was uniform, and its temperature was low because the protosun had not yet begun to radiate as a result of gravitation contraction. This cold nebula began to break up and concentrate into separate masses—the protoplanets, or planets-to-be. Eventually the material at the center (the protosun) became concentrated under the force of gravitation. As it shrank, it became hotter and hotter. Then radiation from the protosun drove most of the lighter elements (particularly hydrogen and helium) out of the protoplanets and the nebula itself. In each protoplanet, most of the heavier elements such as iron and nickel concentrated to-

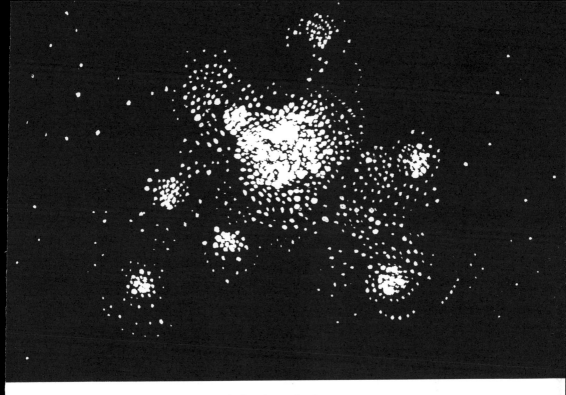

*Kuiper's disk-shaped nebular hypothesis
of the origin of the solar system.*

ward the center. As the protoplanets decreased in size, they began to rotate faster, attaining much the same rotational speed they have today. With this increase in their spinning, material may have been thrown off them, forming satellites.

The other theory now favored by many scientists is the dust-and-gas-cloud hypothesis. According to the American astronomer Fred L. Whipple, who proposed it, the solar system-to-be was at first a vast cloud of cosmic dust and gas. Local irregularities, inevitable in such a dispersed cloud,

15

Whipple's dust-and-gas-cloud hypothesis of the origin of the solar system.

gradually produced rotation and led to the cloud's collapsing inward on itself under its own gravitation. As it did so, the dust and gas became more concentrated. The more solid particles in the cloud collided, stuck together, balled up, and eventually became the planets, while the larger concentration of collapsing gases at the center formed the sun. The present-day planetary satellites may have been smaller fragments that did not merge with the major planets but later became captured in orbits about their parent bodies.

Exactly how the solar system *was* formed is a question that is far from settled. And indeed, just how the natural satellites themselves came into being may forever remain an astronomical mystery. Nevertheless, the moons of our solar system exist, and they are potentially important members of the sun's family.

The Earth and Its Moon

Earth, our home planet, is unique in the solar system for three reasons. It is the only planet known to possess intelligent life. It is the only planet to have large amounts of liquid water on its surface, covering nearly three fourths of its crust. And it is the only planet that possesses a single, relatively large natural satellite, the moon.

As the moon's primary, Earth is the third planet from the sun. Its mean, or average, distance from the sun is about 92,870,000 miles. Earth's period of revolution around the sun, or its year, is 365¼ days, and its rotational period, or day, about its axis is twenty-three hours and fifty-six minutes. Earth's atmosphere, consisting of nitrogen, oxygen, water vapor, and other gases, extends for a depth of 10,000 miles, though after the first 700 miles it becomes very thin. Earth's diameter is nearly 8,000 miles.

Earth is massive. Astronomers use the term *mass* to describe the total amount of matter that a planet contains; it is measured in terms of units such as tons. The mass of Earth is 6 sextillion tons (1 sextillion is the number 1 followed by 21 zeroes.) Compared with Mars, Earth is massive. Mars, though half the size of Earth, is only .11 the mass of Earth. This massiveness of Earth explains in large part why it is able to "hold on" to the moon, which has a diameter of 2,160 miles. The more material there is in a body, the more gravitational attraction it is capable of. By comparison, Mars, with its small mass, could not effectively support a massive moon or moons.

The large size of the moon in relation to Earth makes the Earth-moon system like no other in the solar system. Actually, our moon is only the sixth largest of them all. Three of Jupiter's and one each of Saturn's and Neptune's are larger. But compared to its primary, Earth, the moon is the largest of all.

So large is the moon in relation to Earth that some scientists call the Earth-moon system a double planet. The moon differs from the true planets only in that it orbits around Earth; were it following an independent path about the sun, it would be a full-fledged planet. A viewer of the Earth-moon system from Venus would see it very much as a double planet.

Oddly, the length of the moon's day and its year with respect to its primary are the same. The reason is because its period of rotation on its axis (the day) and its period of revolution around Earth (the year) are equal—twenty-seven Earth days, seven hours, and forty-three minutes. Hence, observers on Earth always see the same side of the moon.

A view of the full moon taken from the Apollo 11 spacecraft at a distance of 10,000 nautical miles from the lunar surface.

Before an unmanned Soviet lunar probe photographed the dark side of the moon in the 1960's, no human being had ever seen it.

The moon is the closest celestial body to Earth, orbiting it at a mean distance of about 239,000 miles. But once each month during its journey around Earth it comes a few thousand miles closer than the mean distance, and once each month it wanders out a few thousand miles farther. The reason for this variation is that the moon travels in an elliptical orbit, or path, around its primary. No known celestial body travels in a perfect circle around its primary, but in an ellipse, an elongated circle.

The moon is visible, as are Earth and other planets, because it reflects the light radiating from the sun. However, the moon is a relatively poor reflector; it reflects only about 7 percent of the sunlight that falls upon it.

The different shapes in which we see the moon in the sky are called its "phases." They are due to the varying amounts of the sunlit lunar surface that we see as the moon revolves about Earth once each month. At full moon, Earth is between the sun and the moon, but the inclination of the moon's orbit to Earth's usually positions the moon outside of Earth's shadow, and the whole lunar disk facing Earth is illuminated. At new moon, the moon is between the sun and Earth, and the sun's rays illuminate only the hemisphere facing the sun, leaving the side facing Earth in complete

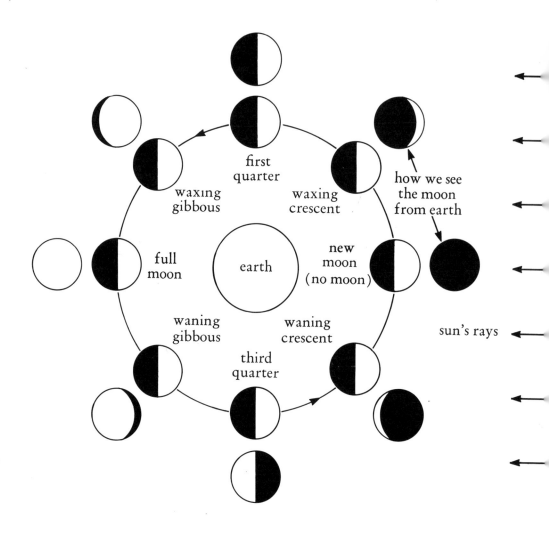

first
quarter

waxing
gibbous

waxing
crescent

how we see
the moon
from earth

full
moon

earth

new
moon
(no moon)

waning
gibbous

waning
crescent

third
quarter

sun's rays

The phases of the moon.

darkness and making it invisible from Earth. After new moon, the waxing, or growing, thin crescent turns into first quarter. Following the full moon, the waning, or lessening, gibbous (humpbacked) phase turns into last quarter, then into new moon again.

To observers on Earth, the motion of the moon occasionally produces two kinds of eclipses. Eclipses of the sun are caused when the moon passes between Earth and the sun and is at or near the point where its orbit crosses Earth's. Then it casts a shadow that extends to Earth. Eclipses of the moon itself are seen when Earth is between the sun and the moon, and the moon is at or near the crossing point of the orbits.

Eclipse of the sun

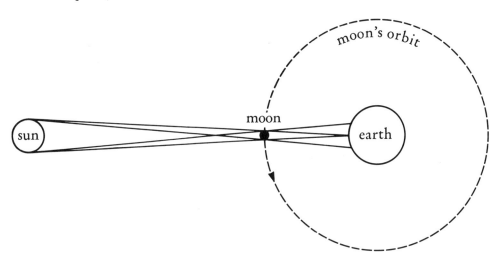

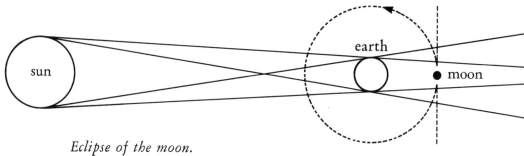

Eclipse of the moon.

The mass of the moon is only ⅟₈₁ that of Earth. Its surface gravity is but ⅙ of Earth, which means that a 150-pound man weighs only 25 pounds on the moon. Because of this reduced gravity the astronauts on the lunar surface seemed to bound and even float along.

Since the moon has no atmosphere, sunlight on the moon is very bright and shadows are absolutely black. Why? Because no blanket of air molecules such as there is on Earth can filter and scatter the sun's rays and insulate the moon as those rays mercilessly beat down on the lunar surface. The lack of atmosphere on the moon also makes its surface temperatures very severe. Near the lunar equator, at noontime, rocks reach 270 degrees Fahrenheit (above the boiling point of water); at midnight, temperatures fall as low as minus 215 degrees Fahrenheit.

As seen through binoculars, the rough lunar surface resembles a ravaged wasteland. It is divided into bright highland areas, comprising about two thirds of the total surface, and dark lowland plains, called "maria" (Latin for "seas") because they were originally thought to be lunar oceans. (The name is actually a misnomer since there is no water on the surface of the moon.)

Craters are the most conspicuous and plentiful of all the moon's surface features. Thousands of them dot the lunar landscape. Some are believed to have resulted from volcanic activity within the moon, and some are doubtless the result of meteoroids and perhaps asteroids impacting on the moon's crust. Craters may also have formed from collapsing material triggered by moonquakes.

Because the craters are far more numerous in the highland areas than in the low lying maria, scientists think that the dark maria developed relatively late in the crater-forming history of the moon. Otherwise, they would contain far more craters than they do. The maria appear to be like giant lava plains that resemble lava beds on Earth.

Rills, or deep canyons, are another feature of the lunar surface. Some are more than 100 miles long. Many scientists believe that these rills were caused by collapsing matter, but at present their origin remains a mystery.

In 1968, small changes of motion in the unmanned Lunar Orbiter 5 spacecraft were picked up by scientists on Earth. These movements revealed the presence of large concentrations of massive material in the moon's crust. The scientists named them *mascons* (after *mass concentrations*). Five con-

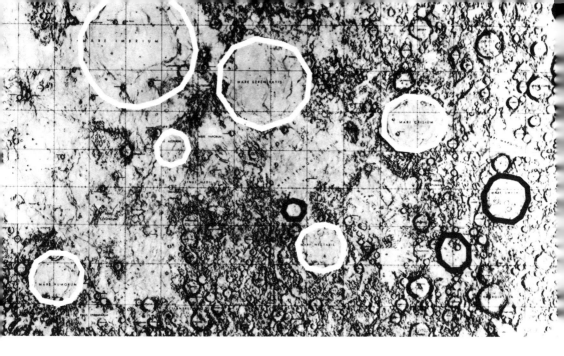

Mascons (ringed in white and black circles)
were discovered through analysis of tracking data
from the Lunar Orbiter missions.

spicuous ones, ranging from 25 to 100 miles in extent and perhaps 25 miles below the surface, were detected under all five large circular maria on the side of the moon facing Earth. Later more mascons were found under other maria by spacecraft orbiting the moon.

Scientists were able to detect these mascons because the spacecraft speeded up as they passed over them. From this observation they concluded that there were larger concentrations of material in these places and that they were exerting stronger gravitational pull on the spacecraft. The

26

extra gravitational pull gave the spacecraft a little extra bit of speed. Yet why, scientists asked themselves, should these large concentrations of matter exist in some places and not in others? Many think that they resulted from the impact of giant meteoroids, which embedded themselves in the lunar surface.

One of the prime missions of the manned landings on the moon by Apollo astronauts was to bring back lunar samples. These valuable collections of moon rocks and soil have been studied now for several years by geologists and other scientists in the hope that they will gain new knowledge of the moon's early history. Some of the specimens already studied are at least half a billion years older than any ever found on Earth.

Specifically, what have been some of the scientific findings from the Apollo landings? Specimens collected from the lunar maria show that some areas are unusually rich in titanium. In addition to titanium, all of the lunar rocks were found to have high concentrations of such rare elements as scandium, zirconium, hafnium, and yttrium, though being deficient in such common Earth elements as chlorine, sodium, and potassium. One lunar area in the Copernicus crater region was found to be especially rich in radioactive uranium and thorium. Fragments of an unusually uranium-rich rock known as KREEP from the Apollo 14 and 15 sites may have been formed very early in lunar history, between

A close-up view of one of the rocks brought back from the Apollo 12 lunar landing. It is a brecchia, a rock composed of angular fragments cemented together.

4.3 and 4.4 billion years ago. Other specimens indicate that the flooding by lava of such lunar seas as the Ocean of Storms and the Sea of Fertility occurred a billion and more years afterward.

The discovery of lunar rocks as old as 4.6 billion years already has cast severe doubts on one long-held theory of the moon's formation. This theory suggests that at one time in the distant past the moon and Earth were a single body rotating at very high speed. So rapid was the rotation that huge quantities of material were torn away from Earth's crust and formed the moon. The great cavity of the Pacific Ocean basin, so states the theory, was the original home of this material. But the oldest known surface rocks on Earth are thought to be only a little more than 3.7 billion years old. If rocks on the moon are known to be as old as 4.6 billion years, how could they have come from Earth? All bodies of the solar system itself are thought to have formed about 4.65 billion years ago.

What does the study of these lunar samples suggest? Why the difference in age between lunar and Earth rocks? Why are such elements as thorium and uranium scarce on Earth and more or less abundant on the moon? The evidence points, some scientists think, to two new variations of the gas-cloud theory of the origin of the moon.

Both these new hypotheses are derived from evidence that the moon is made largely of refractory minerals—those that melt only at very high temperatures, such as thorium, titanium, and uranium. At the time the planets were forming, such substances would have been the first to condense out of the mixture of gaseous compounds thought to have been circling the sun. Substances with lower melting points would have condensed only later as the gases slowly cooled in space.

One of the new theories holds that the moon was formed in an orbital path as close to the sun as that of Mercury, the innermost planet. The theory further suggests that Mercury itself, being so close to the sun, is also formed of refractory materials. An early gravitational battle then ensued between Mercury and the moon. The more powerful gravity of Mercury, a full-fledged planet, eventually threw the moon into a new orbit that carried it out toward Earth. This theory not only accounts for the older rocks of the moon, it explains the greater abundance of refractory minerals in the lunar crust.

The second of the new theories suggests that the moon formed at roughly the same distance from the sun as Earth. But it did so in an orbital path tilted sharply to the plane of the ecliptic, which is the plane of Earth's orbit around the sun. The ecliptic is also the general plane in which the other planets (except Pluto, the outermost) circle the sun —a broad disk-shaped region in which the planets originally formed. Most of the hot gas from which the planets ultimately developed is assumed to have lain in this vast disk. Above and below it, the lower gas temperature and pressure would have allowed refractory minerals to condense and cool first. Thus, the newly evolving moon, which consisted of such material and whose sharply tilted orbit allowed it to escape the ecliptic region for long periods, formed before Earth did.

Whether either of these theories is correct, or whether older ones or variations of them are valid, remains to be seen. Still unanswered is the question of how Earth captured the moon as a satellite and holds it in a relatively circular orbit.

The fifty-odd packages of instruments placed on the lunar surface by the Apollo astronauts have provided scientists with much additional information about the moon also. Each package was somewhat different, but in combination they yielded a great volume and variety of data on cosmic ray behavior, heat flow, seismic waves, and radiation patterns

Astronaut John Young on the lunar surface during the Apollo 16 mission to the moon.

from the sun. All these readings and more were perpetually monitored until the instruments were shut down in 1977, casualties of budget cuts in NASA's space program.

From this wealth of data, scientists found out a number of things they had not known before. Among the most important were discoveries made by NASA's seismographs. For instance, on July 17, 1972, a huge meteorite crashed into the far side of the moon—a relatively rare astronomical event. The seismic waves produced by this impact traveled through the moon and were detected by seismographs on the other side. By interpreting the pattern of these waves—and of other impacts and moonquakes—scientists were able to reconstruct the internal structure of the moon. Other instruments also told scientists about the temperature inside the moon and the distribution of its mass. Meantime, analysis of the moon rocks was suggesting the way in which the moon had developed after its formation.

These combined studies have led experts to believe that the moon's crust is thicker than Earth's. It is about 35 to 60 miles thick while Earth's is only 3 to 30 miles thick. Most of the rest of the moon, they think, is composed of a homogeneous mantle below the crust that extends to within 185 to 310 miles of the center. There may also be an iron core—nonmolten but close to the melting point.

Further analysis of moon rocks brought back from the lunar highlands by the Apollo 16 mission suggests that the

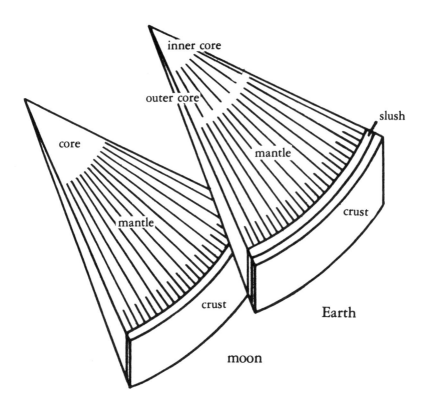

The structure of the moon's interior

moon's crust was formed under intense heat very early in its history—some 4.4 billion years ago. About 100 to 300 million years afterward, asteroids or meteorites, or both, carved out the huge depressions, the maria, in the moon's surface. Then, much later, as the decay of radioactive elements caused the lunar interior to heat up, volcanoes erupted and filled the maria with lava flows.

33

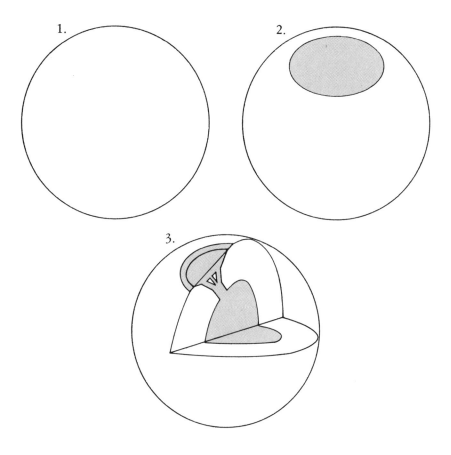

How the seas of the moon were formed

1. Satellite's crust was formed under intense heat some 4.4 billion years ago.
2. About 300 million years later, asteroids or meteorites carved out maria.
3. About 3.2 to 3.8 billion years ago lava from the interior filled the seas.

34

Scientists had not really anticipated this type of evolutionary stage for the moon. But they think it may put our own planetary development in clearer perspective. One NASA scientist suggests there is no reason not to believe that Earth went through a similar series of evolutionary steps. If it did, ideas about the formation of Earth's continents would be subject to revision.

Another NASA scientist believes that the eight-year-long Apollo scientific effort has yielded a "pretty good snapshot of what the Earth will be like as it loses heat, the outer shell thickens, and vulcanism ceases" at some point in the far future. Indeed, he and other scientists believe that what the Apollo Program learned about the moon in a few short years took hundreds of years to find out about Earth.

Mars
and Its Moons

Much of our information about Mars, the fourth planet from the sun at a mean distance of about 141 million miles, has come from the Mariner 9 spacecraft probe, which orbited the planet for almost a year in 1971 and photographed 100 percent of Mars's surface. Mariner 9 returned to Earth information and photographs that have drastically altered scientists' ideas about the body. Some five years later, the Viking landers 1 and 2 set down on Mars on July 20 and September 3, 1976, respectively and materially increased our store of Martian information, particularly of the planet's atmosphere and the possibility of life there.

As observed by Mariner 9, only about half of the Martian surface, chiefly in the southern hemisphere, is substantially cratered. In the northern hemisphere, four huge volcanic mountains were found as well as a vast system of canyons, tributary gullies, and narrow channels—all far larger in scale than anything seen on Earth. The biggest volcanic mountain in the solar system, so far as is known now, is Olympus Mons on Mars; it is 300 miles in diameter at its base and stands 16 miles high (Mount Everest on Earth is

A spectacular picture of the Martian landscape taken by the Viking 1 lander. Sharp dune crests indicate recent windstorms. The meteorology boom, which supports Viking's miniature weather station, cuts through the center of the photograph.

barely 6 miles high). Other spectacular geological features on Mars include a Martian grand canyon that dwarfs the one on Earth.

Mariner 9's cameras also recorded what appeared to be dried-up riverbeds, suggesting the onetime presence of water on the planet. Great channels hundreds of miles long also seemed to have been cut by large amounts of flowing water. Since then the Viking landers have shown that flowing water was significant in shaping the early features of Mars. Furthermore, photographs returned to Earth in 1979 by Viking 2 show water, frozen out of the atmosphere, on the

Martian surface; whether it is frost or snow scientists aren't sure. But they believe there is much water beneath the planet's surface.

As analyzed by the Viking landers, the thin Martian atmosphere contains 95 percent carbon dioxide, 2.7 percent nitrogen, 1.6 percent argon, and traces of oxygen and water vapor. When the Martian winds become really strong, the lower atmosphere can be choked with the dry, reddish dust covering most of the planet's desertlike surface. In 1971, when the Mariner 9 probe reached Mars, the greatest dust storm in more than a century was raging there.

Mars's polar caps appear as a white cover over its north and south poles. This cover grows and recedes with the Martian seasons. Previously it was thought that the caps were frozen carbon dioxide (CO_2), but information sent back by the Viking spacecraft indicates that they are predominantly water ice. In addition, Viking instruments have shown that the average temperature of the whole planet is minus 45 degrees Fahrenheit, with a maximum noontime temperature at the equator of 80 degrees. Such a great variation in temperature indicates that the Martian atmosphere is extremely thin and thus does not retain the sun's heat as Earth's atmosphere does.

The two Viking landers were the first spacecraft ever sent to another planet with equipment specifically designed to search for alien life forms. Viking 1 landed near an area heavily scoured by what are believed to have been ancient floods. Viking 2 is located on the Utopian Plains, which are less pockmarked by craters. Information from biological experiments on Mars are still inconclusive but could suggest, as one NASA scientist put it, "the possibility of biological activity" in the samples being studied. Thus far, however, no such activity has been found. But if life does exist on Mars, it has made a different adaptation than have life forms on Earth.

So Mars, as seen through the eyes of its Viking landers, is a parched, arid, rock-strewn world—a world of dust that often tints its sky red during the savage wind storms that swirl and rage above its ancient volcanoes, craters, and fantastic canyons. As seen from Earth, the red planet Mars reminded the Romans of blood, and so they named it after their god of war. Actually, the dry pinkish dust covering

A photograph of the Martian surface taken by Viking Lander 2 at its Utopia Planitia site in 1979. It shows a thin coating of water ice on the rocks and soil.

most of the Martian surface and giving it a reddish appearance is composed of iron-rich clay and carbonate minerals that have oxidized, or rusted.

Mars rotates eastward on its axis once every twenty-four hours and thirty-seven minutes, which gives it a day that is very nearly the same as an Earth day. The planet takes 687 of our days to complete one revolution around the sun. Thus, a year on Mars lasts almost twice as long as a year on Earth. The Red Planet moves through space somewhat more slowly than Earth does—at about fifteen miles a second—and travels in a more elliptical orbit.

One of the smaller planets in the sun's family, Mars has a diameter of about 4,140 miles, which is a little more than half Earth's diameter. Like Earth, Mars is made up of rocky material. But even if Mars were the same size as Earth, it would not be as massive, which is why scientists describe Mars as less dense than Earth.

Understanding the meaning of density is important. Density is the amount of matter in a unit volume of a substance. Suppose there were two hypothetical planets, A and B. A is made of solid steel; B is made of cork. If one cubic mile were cut out of each planet, both cubes would occupy the same space. But obviously they would not have the same mass. The cube cut from the steel planet would weigh many times more than the cube cut from the cork planet. Or, as scientists say, the steel cube has greater density than the cork one. And the steel planet has greater density than the one of cork.

To make density comparisons more practical, scientists use the density of water as a basis. The density of water is taken as unity, or 1. Thus, the density of Earth has been computed to be 5.5 grams per cubic centimeter, which means that it is 5.5 times as dense as water. The density of the sun is low, only 1.4 that of water. The density of the moon is 3.3.

As for Mars, its density is 3.96 that of water, which is only about 70 percent that of Earth. The reason for this lower density may be that Mars contains a much smaller amount of iron than Earth.

Since Mars is less massive than Earth, it has a much weaker gravitational pull on an object on its surface. The figure for Martian surface gravity is .38, which means that bodies or objects on Mars weigh only 38 percent of what they do on Earth. (Here Earth is taken as unity, or 1, as a basis for comparison.) Thus, a 100-pound earthman would weigh only 38 pounds on the Red Planet.

Mariner 9 cameras radioed back to Earth in November, 1971, the first pictures of two tiny satellites: Deimos and Phobos. Curiously, these moons were objects of interest even before they were discovered in 1877.

In 1610, the German astronomer Johannes Kepler predicted by mathematical means that Mars might have two satellites. However, in his day there were no telescopes powerful enough to pick them up. Yet so sure was Kepler of his prediction that he wrote to the great Italian scientist Galileo of the probable existence of the satellites. Later the French author Voltaire, in one of his imaginative works, also mentioned Mars as having two moons.

Two photographs of Mars taken by Mariner 9.
Top: *A chasm with branching canyons eroding adjacent plateau lands.* Bottom: *a volcanic mountain.*

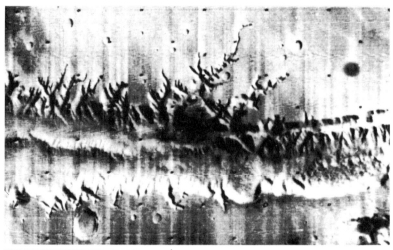

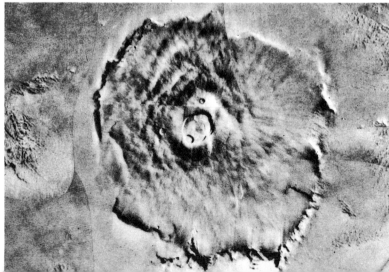

But the most incredible early reference to the two Martian satellites was made by Jonathan Swift in his famous *Gulliver's Travels*, published in the 1720's. In one of Gulliver's adventures, the two Martian satellites are described with a fair amount of accuracy. According to the story, the astronomers of Laputa (an island that was supposed to float above the Earth) "discovered two lesser stars, or satellites, which revolve around Mars, whereof the innermost is distant from the center of the primary planet exactly three of its diameters, and the outermost, five; the former revolves in the space of ten hours, and the latter in twenty-one and a half." Actually, Swift's estimates were too great, for Phobos is only 1.4 times the Martian diameter away from the center of the planet, and the distance of Deimos is only 3.5 diameters. Swift's periods of revolution were off, too. Still, his guesses were astonishingly accurate, considering the fact that the moons were not really sighted until 150 years later.

The actual discoverer of the two moons was Asaph Hall, an American astronomer working at the United States Naval Observatory in Washington, D.C. He was using a twenty-six-inch telescope, then the best in existence. Hall, a master carpenter who used his trade to pay for his education in astronomy, discovered the satellites in 1877.

On the night of August 11, Hall sighted a faint object near the planet. But cloudy weather intervened, and he did not see it again until the sixteenth. Because the object was moving with the planet, there was no doubt it was a satellite and not a faint star. The next night he succeeded in locating another moon even closer to Mars. Hall named the inner satellite Phobos (Fear) and the outer one Deimos (Panic), after the companions of Mars, god of war.

The Viking 1 orbiter provided the first close-up picture of Phobos, the larger of the two moons, in 1977. Both satellites orbit the planet from west to east, which is the usual pattern for other moons in the solar system. Phobos is closer to its primary than any other known satellite in the sun's family. It is only about 5,820 miles from Mars's center, which means that its distance from the Martian surface is approximately 3,750 miles.

Though Phobos is truly a tiny world, only some thirteen miles in diameter, a person on Mars still would be able to see it quite easily in the Martian sky. And it would appear to go through phases just as our moon does. Photographs of Phobos reveal that it has rougher terrain than Deimos. Its most spectacular feature is a six-mile-wide crater, as seen in the accompanying photograph.

Phobos travels around Mars very quickly, taking only seven hours and thirty-nine minutes to complete one orbit. Because Mars is spinning on its axis at a slower rate, Phobos travels around its parent planet faster than Mars itself rotates. Phobos is unique as the only moon in the solar system to do so.

Phobos, photographed by Viking Orbiter 1 in 1978.
Stickney, the largest crater at the left, is six miles across.
In the southern hemisphere, Kepler Ridge casts a shadow that
partially covers the large crater Hall at bottom.

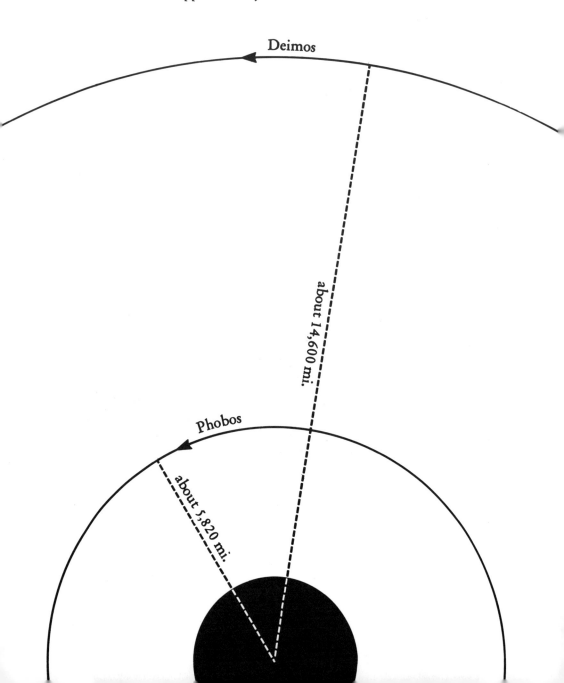

The orbits of Mars's two satellites.
Distances are approximately to scale.

Deimos

about 14,600 mi.

Phobos

about 5,820 mi.

The fact that Phobos is apparently approaching Mars accounts for its short period of revolution. Astronomers think that some 4.5 million years ago its orbital period was about seventeen hours. The chances are that in another 35 or 40 million years Phobos will end its life, either by breaking apart under the gravitational strain of its primary or by crashing into the Martian surface.

The outer satellite, Deimos, is probably no more than seven or eight miles in diameter. The Mariner 9 photographs show that it possesses craters. A person on Mars would not see this miniature world even as a disk. Rather it would look more like a bright star.

Deimos is about 14,600 miles from the center of Mars, much farther than Phobos, and it takes thirty hours and eighteen minutes to orbit Mars once. It revolves around its

Deimos, as photographed by Viking Orbiter 1 at a distance of 2,050 miles. The two largest craters are less than a mile in diameter. Heavily cratered, Deimos is thought to have a very old surface.

parent planet more slowly than Mars itself rotates on its axis. Thus, Deimos would seem to rise reluctantly in the east and set slowly in the west. In fact, so slowly does Deimos move across the Martian sky that before it sets the little moon remains in the sky for more than sixty hours. By comparison, Phobos takes only four and a half hours to cross the Martian sky. Unlike Phobos, Deimos seems to be slowly receding from Mars instead of approaching it.

For most of the Martian year, the two moons would be visible only in the morning or evening twilight, for they would be either invisible against the daytime sky or obscured by the shadow of Mars cast by the sun. Only in midsummer or midwinter would they avoid the shadow long enough to be seen to make an entire trip across the sky. By comparison with our own moon, the masses of these small satellites are tiny indeed. Their gravitational force must be so feeble that an earthman of average weight would weigh only a few ounces on either satellite.

Astronomers are puzzled about the two little moons. Their tiny size and closeness to Mars are hard to explain. How did they get there, and where did they come from? One explanation is that they are captured asteroids. Perhaps during its early history, Mars was able to capture the two bodies as they came within its gravitational pull.

Jupiter
and Its Moons

When Voyagers 1 and 2 made their close approaches to Jupiter in 1979—years after the Pioneer spacecraft had visited there in 1973 and 1974—they radioed back vital information on what has been called the "largest structure in the solar system." For Jupiter is a mighty dynamo that generates vast gravitational and electromagnetic forces that bind it and its many moons into a unique and immense realm: the Jovian system. The great planet embodies within itself alone over 70 percent of all the mass in the planets of the solar system. Indeed, many scientists now look upon Jupiter as the heart of what amounts to a miniature solar system in its own right. Why? Because the planet is a huge, whirling body of gas, in many ways like our star, the sun, and its four rocky inner moons fill the roles of the planets nearer to the sun.

Majestic Jupiter was named for the king of the Roman gods. The fifth planet from the sun, it is by far the largest body in our solar system. Its diameter is a vast 88,000 miles, which is eleven times that of the Earth, and its mean distance from the sun is 484,300,000 miles.

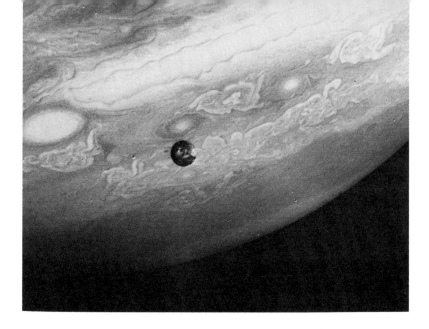

Jupiter's southern hemisphere as photographed in June 1979 by Voyager 2 at a distance of eight million miles away. Seen in front of the turbulent cloud tops is Io, the planet's innermost moon.

Jupiter's orbit lies between the orbits of Mars and Saturn. Its period of revolution is 11.86 years, or nearly 12 of our own Earth years. Considering its huge size, Jupiter spins about its axis unusually swiftly. Its rotational period of only nine hours and fifty minutes makes the Jovian day shorter than that of any other planet in the sun's family. The planet's high rotational speed causes the greater amount of matter at its equator to bulge outward, which, in turn, causes a flattening at the poles.

Unlike Earth and Mars, the giant planet is not solid and rocky. Even before the Pioneer and Voyager encounters, scientists knew about Jupiter's composition for two reasons. First, Jupiter has a very low density, only about 1.34 that of water. Second, scientists had measured the rotational periods of different regions of the planet and found they were spinning in slightly varying lengths of time; some were rotating faster than others. Thus, Jupiter was not rotating about its axis as a solid body, but as a gaseous, loosely knit one.

When Pioneers 10 and 11 flew by Jupiter in 1973 and 1974, they photographed a regularly striped, or banded, world with what appeared to be a well-controlled circulation system. The bands that wrapped the planet were seemingly stable and of several striking colors. Actually, scientists had known for years that Jupiter's visible cloud-topped outer atmosphere was a place of change. But not even the Voyager scientists were prepared for what their spacecraft found in 1979. One scientist put it this way: "The existing atmospheric circulation models have all been shot to hell by Voyager," adding that Jupiter's outer atmosphere is "far more complex in its motions than we have ever imagined."

The Voyager cameras revealed a startling view of a cloud-topped outer atmosphere in violent turmoil. Narrow bands were seen to consolidate and widen; wide stripes were observed to break apart into pieces. Material was transferred between bands instead of adhering to fixed paths in the rapid turbulence. NASA scientists patiently assembled

51

Two photographs of Jupiter taken almost four months apart by Voyagers 1 (left photograph) and 2. They show how the planet's atmosphere undergoes constant change, presenting an ever-shifting face to observers. Note how the white oval spot below and left of the Great Red Spot has drifted eastward (to the right) around the planet. Ganymede is visible at the bottom of the Voyager 1 photo.

"movies" of still photographs that showed the progress of one of the many round spots—hundreds of miles wide—that continually orbit the planet in its atmosphere. It was seen to overtake another spot and roll around it a number of times before it was finally ejected and tossed in another direction.

Nor was this activity all. The Voyager cameras also photographed linear flows of material diverging, whirlpool vortices of brilliant hues reversing direction, and tortuous currents and flows of material lashing the great round spots. Turbulent boundary streams between bands were seen to become knotted riots of color. The cameras' eyes also caught striking reds, blues, yellows, oranges, and browns that made Jupiter's convoluted cloud patterns all the more fantastic. Other complex turbulence patterns between adjacent flows reminded scientists of highly curved saw teeth. And the photographs showed enormous, shimmering auroras—luminous phenomena like Earth's northern lights—larger than

*A close-up of the Great Red Spot taken by Voyager 2 on
July 3, 1979 from 3.7 million miles away.
Note the highly disturbed region west of the Spot.*

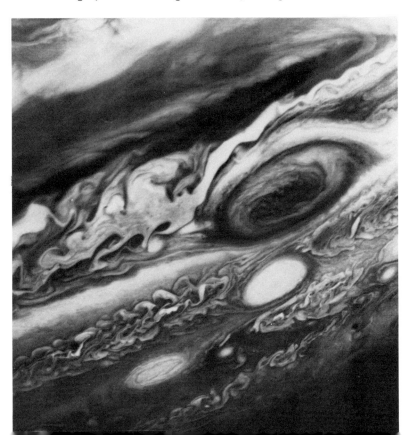

whole planets the size of Earth and Mars. Accompanying them were gigantic flashes, which scientists think were lightning "superbolts."

NASA scientists expressed amazement that, amid such seething turbulence in the Jovian atmosphere, some features have managed to survive for so long. The prime example is the famous Great Red Spot in Jupiter's cloud tops, which is big enough to contain more than a dozen Earths. The Great Red Spot has been known almost since telescopes were first turned toward the planet. But the spot is not always found at the same longitude; it drifts in the roiling atmosphere. Voyager photographs have confirmed it to be an immense circulation system, with its outer clouds swirling counterclockwise at speeds of 200 miles per hour.

Scientists do not yet know the nature of the driving force that keeps the spot intact. They are unsure whether the spot draws its substantive material from its great rim or pulls it up from the depths of the planet's atmosphere and whether the material that keeps the spot surviving is spiraling into or out from its center. When the answer comes, it will bear significantly on understanding the chemistry of the Jovian atmosphere's brilliant colorations.

Other cloud-top features of Jupiter have not survived as well in the violent turmoil of its atmosphere. For instance, three large, white oval spots are all that is left of a white band that circled Jupiter in the 1930's. And smaller features

A Voyager 2 photograph, enlarged, showing the Great Red Spot and the south equatorial belt extending into the equatorial region. An interchange of material between the south equatorial belt and the equatorial zone can be seen at right.

have been observed to change shape in less time than the planet's short period of rotation. One scientist described Jupiter's changing, turbulent outer atmosphere by saying, "You could remap the planet once a week forever and always see a different version."

What material is Jupiter composed of? What makes up its seething cloud tops, and whatever lies beneath them down inside its deep atmosphere? First of all, it should be remembered that earthly observers (and the Voyagers as well) have only seen the tops of Jupiter's clouds. The proportions of actual materials in them and their working chemistry have yet to be unraveled. Voyagers' data will help find the answer, but the best solution will come in the mid-1980's when a diving probe into the Jovian atmosphere, to be called the Galileo mission, is scheduled to gather more information.

Nevertheless, scientists are already fairly well agreed, relying on Earth-based and spacecraft data, that the planet is mostly liquid hydrogen. Perhaps it has an iron core about the size of Earth. Other constituents include helium, methane, ammonia, and heavier elements. The outer clouds are probably ammonia ice crystals, which may become ammonia droplets deeper toward the surface. Temperatures range from perhaps minus 300 degrees Fahrenheit at the top of the cloud decks to some 100,000 degrees Fahrenheit or more down deep at the center. One estimate of the pressure at the center is a crushing 10 million pounds per square inch.

Both Voyager 1 and Voyager 2 carried delicate infrared instruments to measure heat-energy wavelengths emanating from the huge planet. These instruments indicated that heat was leaking out through the blues, browns, and dark red regions of the atmosphere, areas believed to be "holes," or breaks, in the upper cloud decks permitting a view deeper into the thick atmosphere. Also, Earth-based studies have identified "hot spots" through which at least three major cloud levels have been observed: a high, white layer of ammonia crystals; a brownish middle layer; and what may be the deepest "windows" of all, areas of an oddly earthlike blue. Moreover, these "hot spots" have been observed to vary by as much as 40 degrees of temperature in a few Earth days as they change altitude in the spongy, violent Jovian atmosphere.

One of the big surprises of the Voyager 1 flyby in March 1979 was a single photograph showing that Jupiter has a thin ring system of particles surrounding it. At the time the photograph was taken, the camera caught the ring precisely edge-on, and scientists didn't at first detect it. But adjustments in Voyager 2's instrumentation allowed it, in July 1979, to rephotograph the ring a few degrees out-of-plane so that more of it could be seen. The ring appears to be some 15 miles thick, and its outer edge approximately 35,000 miles from the planet's cloud tops. As yet, the ring's particle size and composition are not known, but one NASA scientist thinks that the material inside the main ring element may extend to Jupiter's outer cloud deck.

Another spectacular feature of Jupiter confirmed by the Voyager flybys was its gigantic magnetic field, or magnetosphere, which extends millions of miles out into space. So big is the field that it encompasses all of the planet's major satellites—Io, Europa, Ganymede, and Callisto—and it produces seething radiation belts and other effects. The field links these moons and their huge primary far more intimately

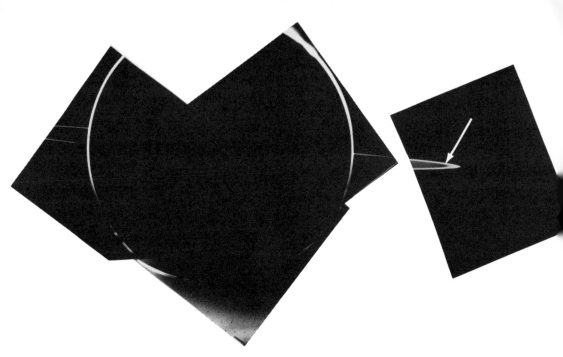

A brilliant halo around Jupiter (arrow)—the thin ring of particles discovered by Voyager 1. The four-picture mosaic was obtained with Voyager 2's wide-angle camera when the spacecraft was 900,000 miles beyond the planet. On each side, the arms of the ring are cut off by the planet's shadow. Viewed from the night side, the planet is outlined by sunlight scattered from a haze layer high in its atmosphere.

than the planet-moon families of Earth or Mars. Just inside the edge of the field, Voyager 1's charged-particle instrument detected what one scientist characterized as the highest temperature in the solar system—300 to 400 million degrees, which is considerably hotter than any part of the sun itself. Outside the immense magnetic field's sunward side is a shock wave, or bow shock, formed where the field abruptly stops the incoming solar wind (charged particles emanating from the sun) and diverts it sharply around the planet.

As may be imagined, Jupiter's mass is high—nearly 317 times that of Earth. Its surface gravity is 2.64 times that of Earth. Thus, a man who weighs 150 pounds on Earth would weigh 396 pounds on Jupiter. With such an increase in weight, a man would find it hard to move about on the surface of the planet, if indeed Jupiter has a well-defined "surface" at all below its chilly, swirling gas clouds.

Despite Jupiter's low density, its great mass gives it the powerful gravitational attraction it needs to "hang on" to one small and four large inner moons and a number of others quite a distance out from the planet.

With its fourteen and possibly more satellites, Jupiter possesses more companions in space than any other major planet. The first to be discovered, in 1610, were the four largest and brightest. They are known as the Galilean satellites because the Italian scientist Galileo Galilei was the man who glimpsed them first.

On January 7, 1610, Galileo happened to turn his homemade telescope toward Jupiter. He was surprised to observe three bright objects near the planet, two on one side and one on the other. The next night he found that the three objects were in different positions, and all were on the same side of Jupiter. As he watched, one of the three "stars"— which is what he first thought them to be—disappeared around the edge of the planet. A few nights later he saw four objects where before there had been three.

Soon Galileo deduced that they must be four natural satellites of the planet. They could not be stars, since all stars are such a great distance from Earth that their movements in the heavens could never appear to be so rapid. Galileo's makeshift telescope was not strong enough to pick up the other Jovian moons. Even so, Galileo could make sufficient measurements to calculate the periods of revolution of the four satellites with surprising accuracy.

Galileo's discovery of the four largest moons of Jupiter came at a favorable time in the history of science. According to Aristotle and other ancient sages, all things including the planets and sun revolved around Earth, which was at rest. Men of Galileo's day still held this belief, although some sixty years earlier the great Polish astronomer Copernicus stated that Earth as well as the planets circled the sun. Galileo's discovery was particularly important because it showed that there could be a center of motion (Jupiter and its moons) that is in turn in motion (as Jupiter itself was known to be around the sun). Up to the time of Galileo's discovery of the Jovian moons, it had been argued that if Earth *were* in motion, the moon would be left behind because it could not keep up with a rapidly moving planet. Yet here were Jupiter's satellites doing just that.

Soon after Galileo's discovery, the same four satellites

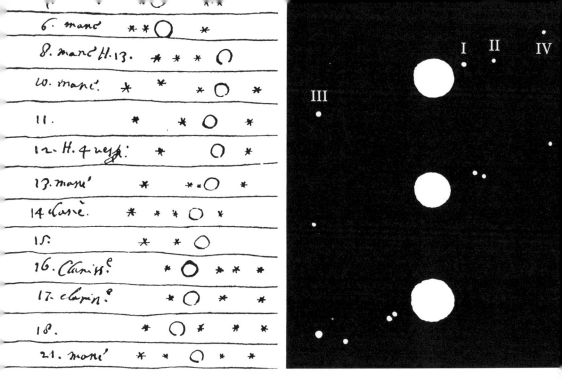

Left: *Galileo's drawings of positions of Jupiter's four large satellites.* Right: *Three exposures showing changes in positions of the four largest and brightest satellites of Jupiter.*

were found independently by Simon Marius, a German astronomer. Marius gave them the mythological names of Io, Europa, Ganymede, and Callisto, in order of increasing distance from Jupiter. These names were not officially recognized until much later; by now they have come into accepted usage. Many astronomers, however, prefer the Roman numeral designations of I, II, III, IV, which were given the Galilean satellites in order of their discovery.

The Roman numeral system was also followed as the re-

61

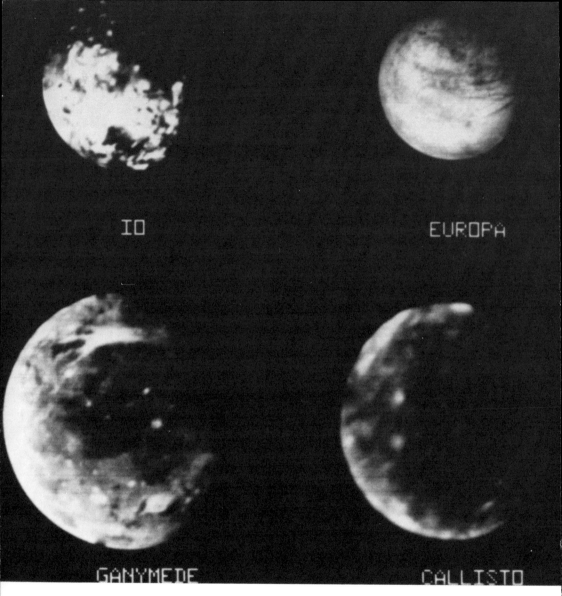

Composite photographs of the four Galilean moons show their correct relative sizes. The two biggest, Ganymede and Callisto, are larger than the planet Mercury, while Io and Europa are about the size of our moon.

62

maining moons were discovered. Due to their greater size and visibility, some were not discovered in order of their distance from Jupiter. The order of the satellites outward from the planet (excluding two recently discovered mini-moons) is: V, I, II, III, IV, VI, VII, X, XII, XI, VIII, and IX.

When using the Roman numeral system, scientists now place the capital letter *J* before a satellite's number; thus, J-III designates Ganymede. In 1974, a thirteenth moon, J-XIII, was discovered, which scientists think may be a captured asteroid. Then, just a year later, Charles Kowal, the astronomer who discovered J-XIII, found yet another tiny Jovian moon—J-XIV. These two minimoons are believed to be each less than five miles wide.

In the mid-1970's, the International Astronomical Union published official names for nine of Jupiter's moons in addition to the four Galileans. J-V, innermost of the Jovian moons, was assigned its already unofficially adopted name of Amalthea. In numerical order (not in order of their distance from Jupiter), J-VI through J-XII are respectively: Himalia, Elara, Pasiphae, Sinope, Lysithea, Carme, and Ananke. Dr. Kowal's choice, Leda, has been suggested for his discovery, J-XIII. J-XIV has yet to be officially named by the IAU.

Jupiter's four largest moons can be seen easily with a small telescope or even with a good pair of binoculars. The two largest, Ganymede and Callisto, are about the size of Mercury (3,100 miles) and would be counted as planets in their own right if they did not revolve around Jupiter.

The four Galileans move about Jupiter in almost circular orbits that are nearly in the same plane as Jupiter's equator and its own orbit around the sun. Since Jupiter's orbit and that of Earth are also nearly in the same plane, the paths of the Galilean moons appear edgewise to observers on Earth. Therefore, the four satellites are seen to swing back and forth from one side of Jupiter to the other, as, in fact, Galileo observed.

Because the Galileans are so nearly in the plane of Jupiter's equator and their periods of revolution are quite short, Jupiter (as observed from Earth) occults, eclipses, or is eclipsed by one or more of the four moons almost daily; only J-IV, because of its greater distance, can sometimes miss. When one of the satellites goes into the shadow of Jupiter, it becomes invisible. This phenomenon is called an "eclipse." When a satellite is hidden by Jupiter itself instead of by its shadow, the event is called an "occultation."

When one of the Galileans passes between the sun and Jupiter, its shadow can be seen easily in a telescope as a black dot moving across the planet's disk. This movement is known as a shadow transit. The transit of a moon itself is more difficult to observe because the moon looks so much like the surface of Jupiter. Due to their vastly greater distance from the primary, the outer Jovian satellites are seen to occult, eclipse, and transit far less often than the Galileans.

As can be seen in the accompanying diagram, Jupiter's moons fall naturally into three distinct groups. The first and innermost group contains the four Galileans and J-V (Amalthea). The latter had escaped discovery until 1892 because of its small size and nearness to the bright planet.

The three satellites in the second group are J-VI, J-VII, and J-X. Orbiting Jupiter at a distance of roughly 7¼ million miles, they all have periods of about 250 days. Their orbits are more elliptical than those of the innermost group and are inclined about 30 degrees to Jupiter's equator.

Moons J-XII, J-XI, J-VIII, and J-IX form the outermost group. All four are about 14 million miles out from the planet and have periods of approximately two Earth years. Their orbits are quite elliptical and are inclined about 150 degrees to Jupiter's equator. The most interesting fact about these outer moons is that their orbital motion is retrograde, or backwards; that is, they do not go from west to east around their primary as do their sister moons, but from east to west. Many astronomers believe this course is no coincidence. They think that these moons are not satellites at all, but asteroids captured by Jupiter's powerful gravitational pull from their original orbits between Mars and Jupiter.

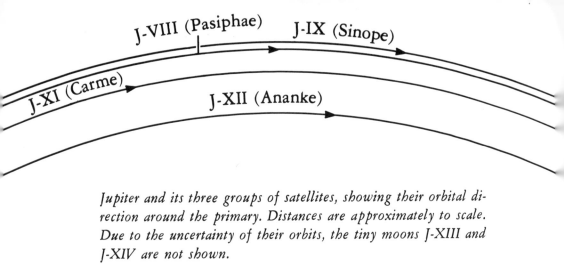

J-VIII (Pasiphae) J-IX (Sinope)

J-XI (Carme) J-XII (Ananke)

Jupiter and its three groups of satellites, showing their orbital direction around the primary. Distances are approximately to scale. Due to the uncertainty of their orbits, the tiny moons J-XIII and J-XIV are not shown.

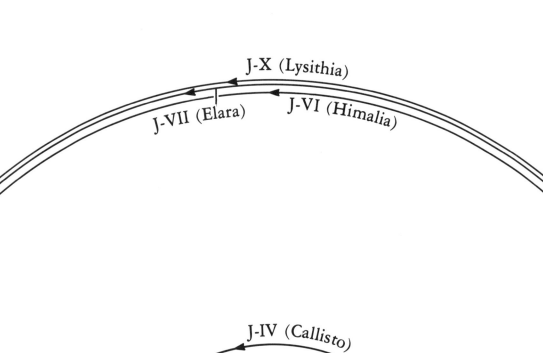

J-X (Lysithia)

J-VII (Elara) J-VI (Himalia)

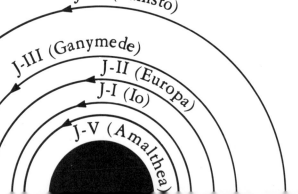

J-IV (Callisto)

J-III (Ganymede)

J-II (Europa)

J-I (Io)

J-V (Amalthea)

Within the two outer groups, the moons' orbits loop through each other. However, the moons in each group move in paths that are so elliptical and angled to each other that they are always a considerable distance apart.

Although the Jovian system constitutes a miniature solar system, scientists have pointed out that, based on the data collected by Voyager 1, Jupiter and its moons do not closely resemble Earth and other planets nearer to the sun—nor do they resemble each other. Voyager 2 reinforced that conclusion. Indeed, planetary specialists reported that they had never seen anything in the entire solar system to compare to the four major Jovian moons—the Galileans—each a distinct world and a source of continuing surprise. Described below, in the order of their increasing distance from the parent planet, are the known moons of Jupiter.

J-V (Amalthea). The Voyager missions produced the first photographs that disclosed anything substantive about the innermost Jovian moon, Amalthea. Tiny, red Amalthea, discovered and named in 1892 by the American astronomer Edward Barnard, whizzes around Jupiter every twelve hours only some 68,000 miles above the planet's cloud deck. With its short period of revolution, J-V has the greatest orbital speed of any known satellite.

Amalthea is strangely elongated, about twice as long (180 miles) as it is wide. Its irregular shape is thought to be the result of a long history of impact cratering. J-V's

67

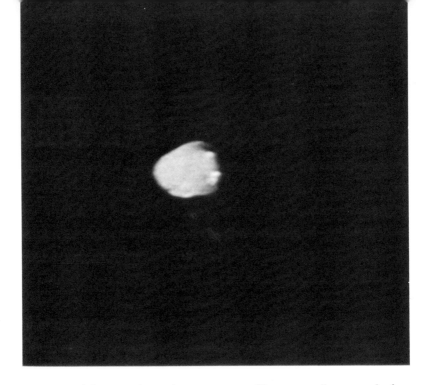

Tiny Amalthea, Jupiter's innermost satellite, was photographed by Voyager 1 at a distance of 225,000 miles. Its irregular shape probably results from a long history of impact cratering.

elongation may also be due to its great velocity and its nearness to Jupiter, subjecting it to tremendous strain. This irregular satellite is thought to keep its long axis pointed toward Jupiter in its motion around the planet so that the spin period around its own axis equals its twelve-hour period of revolution around Jupiter.

J-1 (Io). The innermost of the Galileans, Io takes one Earth day plus eighteen and a half hours to spin around Jupiter. Its distance above the planet's outer clouds at the

Great Red Spot is about 220,000 miles. The satellite is between 2,100 and 2,300 miles in diameter, about the size of Earth's moon.

Prior to the Voyager missions, scientists, when they thought about J-I at all, speculated that Io would be a cold, essentially dead world resembling our moon. Instead, Voyager 1 revealed Io to be a diverse and colorful world—bright orange-red mottled by irregular patches of white. Scientists were amazed to learn that Io was apparently unscarred by any impact craters such as are found on Earth's moon. And they were doubly amazed when they found that Io was alive with active volcanoes. Voyager 1's discovery of still-erupting volcanoes on J-I has been hailed as one of the major findings in the history of planetary exploration by spacecraft.

Studying the Voyager 1 photography, NASA scientists identified eight live volcanoes on Io. Some of the eruptions, greenish in color, sent plumes of gases and other material more than 160 miles above the moon's surface at velocities of over 1,000 miles an hour. For reasons as yet unknown, the volcanoes are distributed around Io's equator. According to measurements taken by Voyager 1, Io's volcanoes seem to be cooler than expected. A chilly world indeed, Io has surface temperatures of about 235 degrees below zero Fahrenheit. One of its volcanic plumes showed a temperature of about 80 degrees above zero. If the volcanoes were vent-

*A full-disk image of Io taken by Voyager 1
from half a million miles away. The circular,
doughnut-shaped feature in the center
is one of the moon's volcanoes.*

ing molten sulfur, as scientists have speculated, the temperature should have been over 200 degrees above zero. This
mystery is only one of many posed by puzzling Io.

Called variously a "weird satellite," "odd moon out," and
a "real mind boggler," Io continues to surprise scientists. For
instance, photographs show signs of more than 100 big depressions that resemble craters, or calderas, of volcanoes on
Earth and Mars. In contrast, however, few of Io's depressions

*A photograph of Io, taken from a distance of 310,000 miles.
The dark, fountainlike feature near the outer edge of the
planet's disk is a volcanic eruption, spewing material some
sixty miles above Io's surface.*

appear to be associated with high domes or other mountain-
ous structures. In fact, the only rugged mountains seen on
Io thus far are chiefly in the polar regions. Another surprise
is that Io appears to be totally lacking in water.

The cause of Io's violent volcanism has yet to be fathomed,
but theories have already been advanced. One proposal is
that a tidal motion is generated in Io's interior by the competing gravitational pull of Jupiter, in one direction, and

Europa and Ganymede in others. Any motion tends to create heat. Such heating could create molten rocky material within the body and periodic eruptions of it at the surface. The tidal heating theory suggests that such volcanism is continuous, with several eruptions going on simultaneously. However, when Voyager 2 reexamined one of the largest vents during the flyby, it appeared to have shut off completely.

A competing theory, based on the fact that Io's surface is very rich in sulfur, suggests that solid rocky material underlying the surface, contains pockets of molten sulfur that extend up and out into a veritable "sulfur ocean" beneath a solid sulfur crust. Sulfur is lighter in liquid than in solid form, and any crack in the crust would allow the liquid to rise—either as a lava flow or an eruption, both of which occur on Io. Either of these theories or variations of them are possible. But then, as scientists are quick to point out, on Io *anything* is possible.

The discovery of a craterless and volcanic Io has led to some fascinating speculations by planetary experts and geologists. One proposal suggests that, judging from lunar studies of the number of craters that ought to have formed through time, Io's currently craterless surface may be astonishingly young—possibly less than 10 million years old, a mere drop in the bucket of geologic time. Another speculation is based on the fact that Io is the first body in the solar

*This picture is one of about 200 images that was used to make
a time-lapse motion picture of Io's volcanic activity.
Note volcanism occurring in Io's upper quadrant.*

system beyond Earth where active volcanism has been observed. Volcanism means comparative youth in a heavenly body. Since the interior of Io has not yet cooled and material still flows and erupts from its surface, this Jovian satellite may have been formed more recently than its sister moons.

Constantly bombarded by electrically charged particles trapped in Jupiter's enormous magnetosphere, Io is wrapped in a glowing veil of sodium atoms, which the Voyager's instruments studied thoroughly. The spiraling of beams of super energetic electrons around the intense magnetic lines of force between Jupiter and Io is probably what produces the fantastic auroral effects photographed by the Voyagers.

Io had yet another surprise for NASA scientists: what seemed to be "blue snow." A recent reexamination of Io photographs disclosed thirty or more wisps of blue material, primarily in the polar regions, which scientists believed to be venting gases that condensed into the "blue snow."

J-II (Europa). The smallest of the Galileans, Europa has an estimated diameter of less than 2,000 miles. It is the only Galilean that is smaller than our own moon. Earth-based estimates show its density to be quite high—4.1 compared to water. The moon takes one Earth day plus eighteen and a half hours to orbit Jupiter. Its mean distance from the planet is about 260,000 miles.

Although Voyager 1 did not make a close approach to Europa, the cameras were able to see enough to show that it was a much different place from Io. The most distinctive features that could be made out in the moon's pale reflected light were long, twisted streaks or tracks crisscrossing the body's surface. Some were estimated to be 100 miles wide and over 1,000 miles long.

When Voyager 2 took close-ups of Europa several weeks later, the complicated linear features appeared even more like cracks or huge fractures in the moon's surface. Also seen in the photographs were somewhat darker, mottled regions, which appear to have a slightly pitted appearance, perhaps due to small-scale craters. No large craters were easily identifiable in the Europa photographs, suggesting that the surface of the satellite is younger than that of Callisto and Ganymede, though not perhaps as young as Io's.

Scientists are fascinated by Europa's strange, wide, rambling, linear features, apparently flush to its surface. One expert described them as "remarkably like the Orwellian drawings of Mars." Most of these dark markings, declared another, are so flat that they could have been "drawn with a felt-tip pen." The surface of the moon appears cracked or broken on a variety of size scales, much in the fashion of pack ice on a sea that is frozen over. Indeed, several NASA scientists believe this analogy is an apt one. They think it entirely possible that Europa's surface is a thin ice crust overlying water or softer ice and that the fracture systems seen are breaks in that crust. Resurfacing mechanisms

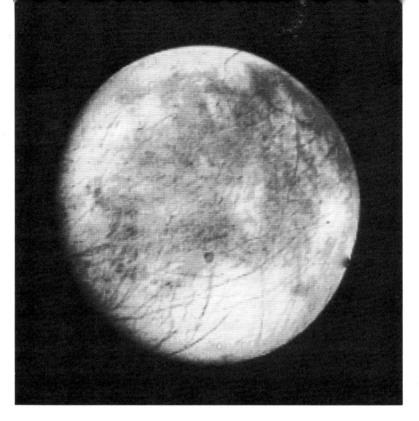

A full-disk photograph of Europa, the smallest Galilean satellite, taken by Voyager 1 from 1.2 million miles away. Note the systems of long linear fractures and faults that crisscross the moon's surface.

such as production of fresh ice or snow along the cracks and cold glacierlike flows are also being considered as possible reasons for the lack of craters.

Yet scientists question what gave rise to the faultlike breaks and cracks in Europa's surface in the first place. One theory is that the tidal process that some scientists propose to account for Io's volcanic activity may also affect Europa,

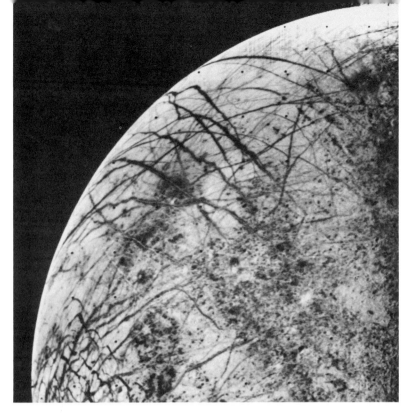

The first close look ever obtained of Europa was photographed on July 9, 1979, by Voyager 2, at a range of 152,000 miles. The surface fracturing and faulting are readily apparent in this picture. Note the absence of large craters.

although on a lesser scale. The tidal pull of Jupiter and its sister satellites might produce stresses on Europa's ice crust either directly or from beneath. Such stresses might periodically force the icy crust apart, creating the faulting and cracking.

Although the area surveyed by Voyager 2 seemed at first to be utterly smooth, further study of the photographs revealed that Europa is not entirely flat. There are some indications of apparent "sagging" of the ice crust, which may be due to heated areas underneath it. And, in addition to the pitted areas, there are some light-colored streaks. Unlike the more predominant dark faults, these streaks seem to be elevated a few feet above the surrounding area. One geologist says they could be regions where relatively purer, whiter ice has risen up through adjacent ice mixed with rocky material.

J-III (Ganymede). With a diameter of nearly 3,400 miles, Ganymede is larger than the planet Mercury and is the largest of the four Galilean satellites of Jupiter. At a mean distance of some 664,000 miles from its primary, Ganymede takes seven Earth days, three hours, and forty-three minutes to orbit Jupiter. It has a low density—about half that of our moon—and is probably composed of a mixture of watery ice and rock. In fact, it may be 50 percent water by weight.

Ganymede received Voyager 2's closest scrutiny of the whole mission when the probe swept past it at a distance of barely 38,000 miles. Voyager 1, which photographed the opposite side of the moon, had already found that Ganymede has numerous parallel faults, some lined up in swaths more than fifty miles wide. In some places the swaths are broken and offset by what appears to be transverse faulting. Some of these faults seem to meet in patterns of surprisingly regular right angles. Ganymede's surface is also heavily pockmarked with ancient impact craters that bear some resemblance to our moon's. In addition, there are regions of what look like lunar maria. Portions of Ganymede's cratered terrain appear to overlie the remains of huge multi-ringed basins—evidences of very ancient events that occurred on a titanic scale. One huge circular area is so thoroughly pounded with impact markings that it looks, in the words of one scientist, like a "piece of Callisto," which shows the effects of heavy meteorite bombardment.

If scientists' early speculations are correct, the discovery

Ganymede, Jupiter's largest moon, as photographed by Voyager 1 from 1.6 million miles away. Large, dark features resemble maria on our own moon.

of the right-angled, transverse faulting features scattered across the big moon's surface is one of Voyager's major achievements. To them, these features suggest that hundreds of miles of crustal movement have taken place—apparently the same kind of internal heavings that give rise to Earth's own plate-tectonic motions. So far, Ganymede has been the only extraterrestrial body to exhibit this kind of crustal movement. Thus, if the theories are valid, Ganymede can

A striking close-up of Ganymede's surface taken from about 150,000 miles away. The most outstanding features are the bright ray craters. The moon contains large amounts of surface ice.

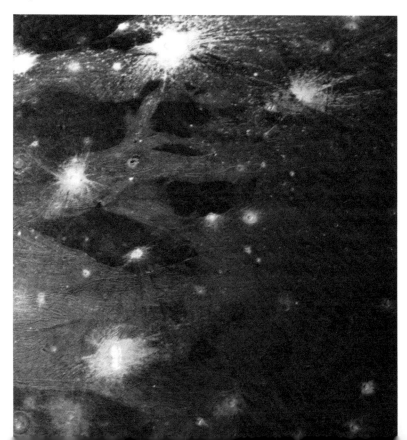

provide scientists with a ready-made mirror of Earth's own ancient developmental past.

J-IV (Callisto). Second largest and outermost of the Galileans, Callisto is a little smaller than Ganymede, about the size of the planet Mercury. Circling Jupiter at a mean distance of about 1,170,000 miles, Callisto has a period of revolution that is sixteen Earth days, sixteen hours, and thirty-two minutes. Like Ganymede, the moon is a low-density ice world.

Callisto is apparently composed of a mixture of ice and rock. Its darker color (about half as reflective as Ganymede's) suggests that its upper surface is "dirty ice" or water-rich rock frozen at the moon's cold surface—about 240 degrees below zero Fahrenheit at the equator.

Callisto may turn out to be a special kind of showcase for planetologists. Since the early days of spacecraft research, scientists have hoped to find and photograph worlds with "pristine surfaces"—areas of heavenly bodies whose appearance preserves a record of the heavy meteorite bombardment in the early days of the solar system. Callisto may be such a world, for scientists believe it may be the most heavily cratered body in the solar system. A few such pristine surface areas exist on our own moon and some on Mercury, but most such regions have been covered up by more recent lava floodings and other processes. Callisto however, said one scientist, "doesn't look like anything has happened to it

The moon Callisto photographed by Voyager 2 at a distance of 677,000 miles. The most heavily cratered of the Galileans, it resembles ancient crater terrain on the moon and Mars. Bright areas are ejecta thrown out by relatively young impact craters.

since the end of the final stages of accretion," by which he meant the formation of the body. If so, Callisto would amount to an actual museum of conditions 4 to 4.5 billion years ago.

What puzzles scientists about Callisto, however, is the lack of craggy topography that such an intense bombardment would have left behind it. High crater walls and

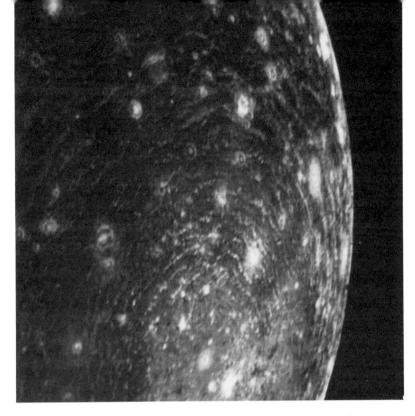

A world of ice and rock, Callisto was photographed at close range—about 220,000 miles—by Voyager 1. The prominent bull's-eye feature is believed to be a large impact basin similar to the Oriental Sea on the moon.

towering central peaks, for example, that are typical of rocky worlds like our moon are virtually absent on Callisto. Yet scientists have a possible explanation for this phenomenon. Since Callisto may be as much as half ice, the slow glacial flowing of the ice may well have erased most of those vertical relief features in a tiny fraction of the moon's lifetime—possibly less than 1,000 years.

The enormous ringed bull's-eye type of feature—the most prominent on Callisto—shown in the close-up photograph on page 83 is believed to be a giant impact basin, similar to the Oriental Sea on the moon. Its outer ring is about 1,600 miles across. The presence of this great impact basin supports the theory that Callisto's surface is ancient.

J-VI (Himalia). Himalia was discovered in 1904 by the French astronomer Charles Perrine. At a mean distance of about 7,130,000 miles from Jupiter, it revolves around the planet in about 250 Earth days. Estimates of its diameter range all the way from 30 to 100 miles. However, J-VI is by far the largest of the outer Jovian moons. No sound estimates have been made of its density or composition.

J-VII (Elara). Elara was discovered by Perrine in 1905. Estimates of its diameter range widely—from as small as 6 miles to as high as 35 miles. At a mean distance of about 7,300,000 miles from its primary, J-VII orbits Jupiter in about 259 Earth days. Its density and physical composition are unknown.

J-X (Lysithia). The American astronomer S. B. Nicholson discovered Lysithia in 1938. Among the smallest of Jupiter's moons, it has a diameter estimated to be from 4 to 15 miles. J-X revolves about Jupiter at a mean distance of about 7,300,000 miles and takes 259 days to make one revolution. Neither its density nor its composition is known.

J-XII (Ananke). Discovered in 1951 by Nicholson, J-XII

revolves in retrograde motion about Jupiter at a mean distance of about 13,000,000 miles and does so once every 631 Earth days. It may be the smallest of Jupiter's satellites, with estimates of its diameter ranging from 4 to 14 miles. Its density and composition are unknown.

J-XI (Carme). This tiny moon was discovered by Nicholson in 1938. It revolves in retrograde motion around Jupiter at a mean distance of about 14,000,000 miles, making one complete revolution in about 692 days. Estimates of its diameter range between 6 and 19 miles. Its density and composition are unknown.

J-VIII (Pasiphae). Pasiphae was first seen by P. J. Melotte, in England, in 1908. It travels in retrograde motion around its primary at a mean distance of about 14,600,000 miles. Its period of revolution is about 740 days. Estimates of its diameter run from 9 miles to 35 miles. Nothing is known of its density or composition.

J-IX (Sinope). Sinope, the outermost of all the Jovian moons, was discovered by Nicholson in 1914. Orbiting its primary at an immense mean distance of some 14,700,000 miles, J-IX takes 758 Earth days to complete its journey around Jupiter, and it travels in retrograde motion. Estimates of its diameter run from 6 to 17 miles. Nothing is known of its density or composition.

Saturn
and Its Moons

As the tiny Pioneer 11 space probe—launched so long before in 1973—sped away from Saturn on September 3, 1979, away from the giant moon Titan, and out of the planet's huge magnetic sphere, it had already made history by becoming the first spacecraft to make a reconaissance of the Saturnian environs. Weighing only 570 pounds, Pioneer 11 had dipped precariously under the rings of Saturn and flown to within 13,000 miles of the planet's cloud tops.

Scientists on Earth were soon reporting that pictures sent back by Pioneer revealed the presence of two previously unknown rings around Saturn as well as a hitherto undetected gap between two of the brightest rings. The spacecraft also spotted not one but two new moons orbiting the giant planet.

Beautiful, ringed Saturn is the sixth planet from the sun. Second only to Jupiter in size, Saturn has a diameter of 75,000 miles, or nine and a half times that of the Earth. This giant body takes twenty-nine and a half Earth years to complete one revolution around the sun. It rotates on its axis only slightly less rapidly than Jupiter, completing a day

One of the earliest views of Saturn, taken by Pioneer 11's cameras on August 21, 1979. The spacecraft was approximately 5.8 million miles from the planet. At lower right can be seen Titan, Saturn's largest satellite. Note the shadow of the ring system cast on the planet's disk.

in only ten Earth hours and fourteen minutes. It revolves about the sun at a mean distance of 886 million miles.

Saturn's mass, though ninety-five times greater than Earth's, is low for its size. Its density is only .71 that of water. Saturn is the least dense of all the planets. Thus, if there were an ocean big enough to hold it, Saturn would float in water! Saturn's low mass causes its surface gravity to be low—only 1.13 that of Earth. Should an earthman be transferred to the Saturnian surface, he would find his weight only slightly increased.

Like Jupiter, Saturn does not rotate as a solid body but as a gaseous, loosely knit one, and its rapid rotation produces a bulge at the equator and a corresponding flattening at the poles. So distant is the planet from the sun that it receives only $\frac{1}{90}$ of the sunlight per unit area that Earth does.

Data from Pioneer 11 seems to support what scientists, using Earth-based information, had suspected about Saturn's interior and atmosphere. Their theory is that the planet has a rocky inner core about the size of Earth but three times its mass. Around the core is wrapped a compressed blanket of such materials as water, methane, and ammonia. Extending farther out from the core is a thick layer of electrically conductive metallic hydrogen, whose currents are the source of the planet's magnetic field. Most of the rest of Saturn consists of somewhat less dense liquid hydrogen. And surrounding this body is a thin, gaseous layer, forming a cloud-topped atmosphere.

By comparison with the tumultuous outer atmosphere of Jupiter, Saturn is a rather smooth and bland-faced world. Part of the reason lies in its lower temperatures (it is twice Jupiter's distance from the sun), which allow for the formation of high-altitude hazes of chemicals such as ammonia. Scientists think that such a haze would tend to conceal a

*Saturn as photographed by Pioneer 11 at a distance of about
1.5 million miles. The planet's banded structure is apparent in
this picture. The moon Rhea, sixth out from Saturn's cloud tops,
can be seen as a speck of light below the planet. It is about
half the size of Earth's moon.*

more dramatic, Jupiter-type color scheme that could exist
below. Additional Pioneer data seems to confirm Earth-
based information that Saturn's internal heating causes it
to emit about 2.5 times as much energy as it receives from
the sun. This phenomenon, scientists think, may be caused
when Saturn's magnetic waves meet the solar wind (radiation) at the outer edge of Saturn's magnetic field and are
deflected back to the planet. However, Saturn's magnetic
field, though large, is three to five times weaker than
scientists expected.

Saturn owes both its beauty and uniqueness in the sun's

family to its spectacular system of rings. They were first seen by Galileo in the same year that he discovered the four large Jovian moons.

As observed from Earth, the ring system is chiefly in three concentric parts. The innermost section is known as the crepe ring, or C ring; the next section is the bright, or B, ring; the outermost is the A ring. Because it is faint, the crepe ring can be seen only in large telescopes and was unknown before 1850. The 2500-mile gap between the A and B rings is called Cassini's Division in honor of the astronomer C. D. Cassini, who was the first to see and describe it in 1675. Late in 1969, Pierre Guerin, a French scientist, discovered a fourth, faint ring, D, inside the crepe ring. Then, in the 1970's, a very faint E ring was discovered, extending from the outside of A to a distance estimated to be as great as fifty times the radius of Saturn.

However, Pioneer 11's flyby in 1979 added new detail to the already complicated picture of Saturn's ring structure. Pioneer detected an F ring about 2,000 miles outside the clearly visible ring system, and an even fainter G ring that seems to occupy a region about 400,000 to 600,000 miles above the equatorial cloud tops. The E ring is so rarefied that Pioneer did not even detect it with its instruments but it has been inferred from Earth-based measurements and possibly extends outward from the main rings for a distance of some 2 million miles. The gap between the faint new F

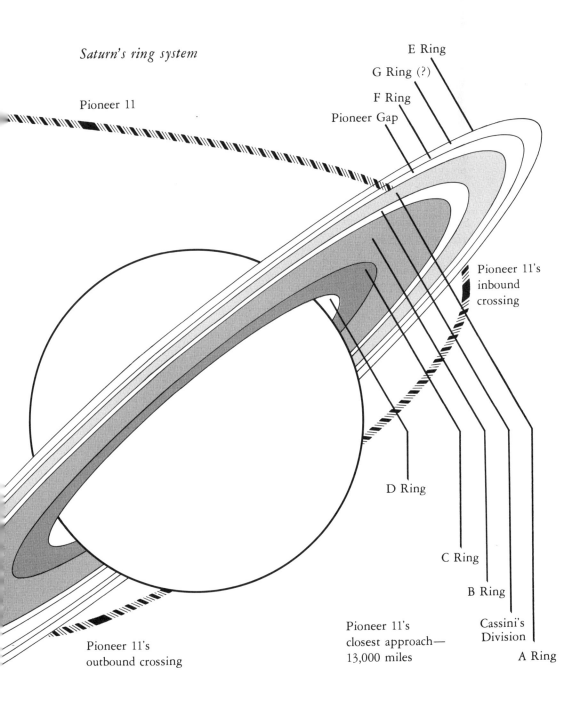

Saturn's ring system

Pioneer 11

E Ring

G Ring (?)

F Ring

Pioneer Gap

Pioneer 11's
inbound
crossing

D Ring

Pioneer 11's
outbound crossing

Pioneer 11's
closest approach—
13,000 miles

C Ring

B Ring

Cassini's
Division

A Ring

Saturn's ring system and its shadow are seen in this view from Pioneer 11 when the spacecraft was within 971,200 miles from its first encounter with the planet. The photograph was made on August 21, 1979, one day before Pioneer 11 reached Saturn.

ring and the much more prominent A ring has been informally christened the Pioneer Division in honor of the spacecraft.

Many scientists have assumed that the ring particles are composed largely of water ice. The new Pioneer information seems to support this view. Gravitational data, for instance, suggest that the rings have a low overall mass, as they would if they were mostly ice. Pioneer measurements also provide clues as to the rings' structure. The temperature difference between the ring system's shadowed and sunlit sides is great enough to suggest that the rings are more than a single layer of particles thick, as some researchers had previously thought.

The rings lie exactly in the plane of Saturn's equator. However, unlike Jupiter's axis, which has very little tilt, Saturn's has a large tilt of 28 degrees to the orbit of Earth

Two frames of Saturn taken by Pioneer 11 on the day of its closest encounter with the planet, September 1, 1979. The spacecraft was about 245,000 miles from Saturn. Cassini's Division, which divides the outer A ring from the B ring, can be seen clearly in this photograph.

(used as a basis for comparison). Because of Saturn's tilt, an observer on Earth seems to see the rings change from a straight line, when viewed edgewise, to a full circle as Saturn goes through its twenty-nine-and-a-half-year period of revolution. One proof of the thinness of the rings is that they cannot be seen even in powerful telescopes when they are edgewise to Earth as during 1980. The accompanying diagram shows the changing aspects of Saturn's rings.

The origin of Saturn's rings has puzzled astronomers for many years. Some think they may be due to a former satellite that came too close to the planet and broke up under the stress of its gravitational attraction. Others think it equally as likely that the ring particles are merely material that never came together to form one body.

Besides the countless tiny satellites that comprise Saturn's rings, a number of moons of a more orthodox variety orbit the big planet. Before 1966, it was thought there were only nine, but in that year when there was an edgewise presentation of Saturn's rings, the tenth, Janus, was discovered.

Janus had been considered the innermost satellite, until Pioneer 11 discovered a new moon about 56,000 miles out from Saturn's cloud tops, and thus 4,000 miles inside the orbit of Janus. The new moon did not come as a surprise to scientists. Because of the proximity of the bright rings, Janus has been seen in only a few telescopic photographs from Earth. While trying to see Janus again in the late

1970's, some astronomers thought they detected a "ghost" of Janus, another object nearby. Since no one could agree on what had been seen, the object was simply recorded as S-11, or a probable eleventh moon of Saturn.

When scientists checked their data after Pioneer's flyby,

Left: Saturn, photographed at the Lowell Observatory, Flagstaff, Arizona. Right: Saturn's changing rings as they appear from Earth.

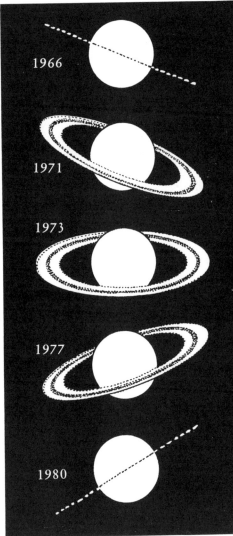

1941

1943

1945

1966

1971

1973

1977

1980

they found confirming evidence of a moon having a diameter of about 375 miles at the most. Magnetic data indicated that it has some degree of electric conductivity, characteristic of metallic objects or, more probably, of ice. One of Pioneer's photographs of Saturn included a speck of light in a position that suggests it may be this new moon. It was then decided that the discovery would no longer be listed as simply S-11, but as 1979 S-1, or the first satellite of Saturn discovered in 1979. In addition, Pioneer's instruments detected another moon, informally christened Pioneer Rock, which may be about the size of 1979 S-1; however, its orbit is as yet imperfectly known.

The known Saturnian moons were discovered generally in order of their largeness and brightness. Fortunately, the confusing system of Roman numerals was avoided in favor of naming them after mythological characters. The innermost moon is 1979 S-1, and next comes Janus. After Janus, in increasing distance from their primary, come Mimas, Enceladus, Tethys, Dione, Rhea, Titan, Hyperion, Iapetus, and finally Phoebe.

The innermost satellites form a distinct group, all having nearly circular orbits in the same plane as Saturn's rings. Farther out, the largest (Titan) and the second smallest (Hyperion) are more or less companions, with orbits within less than 200,000 miles of each other. Much farther out is Iapetus, and the most remote is Phoebe, each circling Saturn

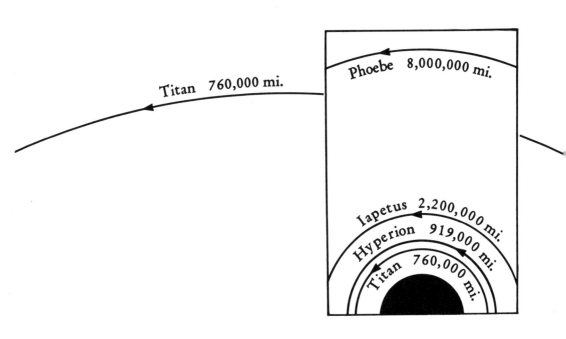

Phoebe   8,000,000 mi.

Titan   760,000 mi.

Iapetus   2,200,000 mi.

Hyperion   919,000 mi.

Titan   760,000 mi.

Orbits of the Saturnian satellites. Inset shows the great distance of Phoebe, even from its nearest neighbor, Iapetus. Distances are approximately to scale.

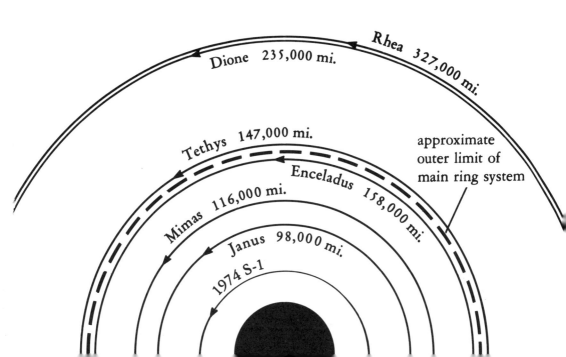

Rhea   327,000 mi.

Dione   235,000 mi.

Tethys   147,000 mi.

approximate outer limit of main ring system

Enceladus   158,000 mi.

Mimas   116,000 mi.

Janus   98,000 mi.

1974 S-1

in lonely orbits millions of miles from their primary. Some astronomers believe that all of Saturn's moons rotate on their axes so as to present the same face to the planet, as our moon does to Earth.

The Saturnian satellites (except for 1979 S-1 and Pioneer Rock, about which next to nothing is known) are described below in the order of their increasing distance from the planet.

Janus. Discovered by the French astronomer Audouin Dollfus in 1966, Janus is one of the smallest of Saturn's moons. Its diameter is about 185 miles. Janus orbits the parent planet at a distance of only 98,000 miles, completing one revolution in about eighteen hours. So close is Janus to Saturn that it is highly elusive. Dollfus was able to spot it in 1966, because that was a year in which the rings were presented edgewise to Earth and thus virtually out of view. Janus is impossible to observe under any other conditions. The moon's density and composition are unknown.

Mimas. Discovered by the English astronomer Sir William Herschel in 1789, Mimas has a mean distance from the planet that is about 116,000 miles, and it completes one revolution around the primary in twenty-two-and-a-half Earth days. Its diameter is about 300 miles. Mimas may have a density so low that it would float in water. Little is known of its composition except that some astronomers think it is probably icy in nature.

Enceladus. This satellite was also discovered by Herschel at the time he discovered Mimas. At a mean distance of about 158,000 miles from Saturn, it revolves around the parent planet in one day and nine hours. Enceladus's diameter is about 400 miles. Like Mimas, it may have a density less than that of water and its composition may be icy.

Tethys. This moon was discovered by Cassini in 1684. It is larger than Janus, Mimas, and Enceladus, with a diameter of about 600 miles. But like Mimas and Enceladus, it may have a density less than that of water and its composition is probably icy in nature. At a mean distance of about 147,000 miles from Saturn, it revolves around the planet in one day, twenty-one hours, and eighteen minutes.

Dione. Dione was also found by Cassini in 1684. At a mean distance from Saturn of about 235,000 miles, it completes one revolution around the planet in two days, seventeen hours, and forty-one minutes. Its diameter is about 600 miles. With a density approximated at 3.2, which is about the same as our moon's, Dione may be the densest of all Saturnian satellites. Its composition is unknown.

Rhea. Also discovered by Cassini, in 1672, Rhea is larger than any of the other moons whose orbits lie closer to Saturn than its own. Its estimated diameter is about 800 miles. At a mean distance of about 327,000 miles from Saturn, it completes one revolution of the planet in four days, twelve hours, and twenty-five minutes. Its density compared to water is about 1.9. Nothing definite is known of Rhea's composition.

Titan. The greatest of Saturn's moons, Titan is probably the largest satellite in the solar system (Neptune's little-known Triton is the nearest competitor). With a diameter of 3,600 miles, it is almost twice as large as our moon, larger than the planet Mercury, and nearly as large as Mars. But the most remarkable thing about Titan is that it is the only known moon in the solar system to have a significant atmosphere—primarily of methane.

Titan revolves in an almost circular orbit about Saturn at a mean distance of about 760,000 miles, taking about sixteen Earth days. Faint surface details have been detected on Titan's disk with very large telescopes. Its density is about 2.3. The satellite was found by the Dutch astronomer Christian Huygens in 1655.

Brightest of Saturn's moons, Titan was first discovered to have an atmosphere by Kuiper in 1944. Using spectroscopic methods—that is, by analyzing the sunlight reflected from Titan—Kuiper found that the satellite had a thin atmosphere of methane and some ammonia. Until recently, Kuiper and other scientists believed Titan had a forbiddingly low surface temperature, some 180 degrees below zero Fahrenheit. At approximately 900 million miles from the sun, Titan would receive only about 1 percent of the sunlight that Earth gets.

*The moon Titan is seen for the first time by spacecraft
as Pioneer completed its mission to Saturn on September 2, 1979.
In this view, Titan is about 230,000 miles from the probe's
cameras. Pioneer's speed relative to Saturn was about 25,100
miles per hour.*

But in 1972, new findings were announced concerning Titan, which were largely the result of the work by Carl Sagan, an American astronomer, of Cornell University. Most startling of the findings was that Titan's atmosphere is apparently not as cold as scientists previously thought it to be—possibly 90 degrees below zero Fahrenheit at the lowest. Such temperatures are not much colder than those at Earth's North Pole. Because of its temperature and because of certain processes he believes are taking place in the satellite, Sagan thinks that Titan may be hospitable to some form of life in the future. Other scientists besides Sagan are allowing for the possibility that an elementary life form might eventually emerge there.

From the Earth, Titan appears to be blanketed by an opaque orange smog. The particles making up this smog are believed by some scientists to be organic molecules formed by the interaction between sunlight and the big satellite's atmosphere. This phenomenon has given rise to a number of scientific speculations. Could the conditions on Titan be comparable to Earth's primordial atmosphere, out of which life eventually evolved? Could Titan's chemistry be producing more complex organic compounds or even some forms of primitive life? The latter possibility is one that most scientists believe, for the present at least, to be rather remote.

Does Titan's orange smog create a greenhouse effect that warms the satellite's surface? Could the particulate matter from the smog, settling to the surface over eons of time, have created a thick layer of hydrocarbons that could be an energy source to some future interplanetary civilization? Such questions may receive more complete answers when the Voyagers reach Saturn in 1980 and 1981.

During its Saturn encounter, Pioneer 11 took five low-resolution pictures of Titan that showed the orange smog. But the pictures also showed some surprising patches of blue, indicating that the smog may not totally cover the moon. Unfortunately, the measurements that might have begun to resolve some of these speculative questions were, for the most part, lost in the noise of poor radio transmission, much of it due to the interference of solar-wind radiation.

Pioneer's infrared instruments did reveal that Titan apparently has no internal heat source, such as volcanoes, that might warm it and produce more hospitable conditions. But lost were much-anticipated infrared measurements of Titan's day-night temperature difference. Such measurements could have determined whether Titan has a thin and unpromising atmosphere like Mars or a thicker atmosphere that could provide a possible life-sustaining greenhouse effect.

Hyperion. One of the smaller, fainter Saturnian moons, Hyperion was discovered by the American astronomer W. C. Bond in 1848. Its diameter is about 300 miles. Orbiting the primary at a mean distance of about 919,000 miles, it completes one revolution of Saturn in twenty-one days, six hours, and thirty-one minutes. Despite its small size, Hyperion is fairly dense—3.0 compared to water. But nothing definite is known of its composition.

Iapetus. This moon was discovered by Cassini in 1671. Its diameter is about 700 miles. At a mean distance of some 2,200,000 miles from Saturn, it moves slowly in its large orbit, completing one revolution in seventy-nine days and nearly eight hours. Its density and composition are unknown.

Iapetus is one of the most interesting members of Saturn's family, because it varies sharply and strangely in brightness.

When it is west of Saturn, it reflects much more sunlight than it does on the planet's eastern side. Some astronomers think that perhaps the moon has a synchronous rotation on its axis; that is, it spins only once in the same time that it takes to go around Saturn. If so, the brightness variations could be explained by one of its hemispheres reflecting light better than the other. One astronomer suggests that in the remote past Iapetus was either discolored by a gaseous outburst from Saturn or disfigured by a passing celestial body. Other scientists have speculated that it has an atmosphere that freezes when it is behind Saturn and out of the sun. When Iapetus appears on the western side, the sun strikes it on the frozen atmosphere; this highly reflective surface would account for the greater brightness on that side. However, many astronomers do not think Iapetus has an atmosphere, which leads them to believe that the satellite is somehow irregular in shape and thus reflects more light on one of its sides.

Phoebe. The outermost of Saturn's satellites, Phoebe was the first moon in the solar system to be discovered by photographic means instead of by telescope. The American astronomer W. H. Pickering recorded it on photographic plates in 1898. Of the presently known Saturnian moons, Phoebe is the smallest, with a diameter of only about 100 miles. This little moon is so far from Saturn—over 8 million miles—and from Iapetus, its nearest sister, that one astronomer has referred to Phoebe as "antisocial." It takes a leisurely one and a half years to complete one revolution of its primary.

Phoebe further asserts its independence of its sister moons by moving in a retrograde motion around Saturn, that is, from east to west, in the opposite direction from the others. Also, Phoebe's orbit is tilted very sharply away from Saturn's equator, unlike those of the other satellites. Its density and physical composition are unknown.

Uranus
and Its Moons

Far out in the solar system is the seventh planet from the sun, the giant Uranus, which is the fourth largest of the sun's family. Actually the first major planet to be discovered, it was sighted in 1781 by Sir William Herschel. Until then, Saturn had been the outermost of the known planets. Even the ancients had known of Saturn, Jupiter, Mars, Venus, and Mercury, because they could be seen fairly easily with the naked eye.

Uranus, too, can be seen with the naked eye, but before Herschel's observations it had been recorded some twenty times as a star. On the night of March 13, Herschel was observing the stars in the constellation Gemini with a seven-inch telescope he had just made. Suddenly he saw an object that seemed to be a star—but one that showed a disk. Herschel was puzzled, since all true stars are not disks but mere points of light, even when viewed through a telescope.

Observing the unknown celestial body night after night, Herschel noted that it changed position among the stars. Soon he came to the conclusion that this "moving star" was really a comet, and he so described it in the report he sent to the Royal Society, the renowned British scientific body.

Herschel's "comet" was carefully followed by astronomers all over Europe. They noted that it followed an almost circular orbit far outside Saturn's. In time, they came to realize that the new body was indeed a planet, and Herschel was hailed as its discoverer. He named it Georgium Sidus (Georgian Star) after King George III of England. Until about 1850, English astronomers called the planet the Georgian; to others, it was known as Herschel. Its ultimate name—Uranus—was chosen by the German astronomer Johann Bode.

Since there are 5,000 stars in the night sky that appear as bright or brighter, it is not surprising that Uranus escaped notice for so long. The cause of its faintness is its remoteness from the sun—a mean distance of about 1,783,000,000 miles; it is over nineteen times farther from the sun than is Earth. Uranus takes eighty-four Earth years to complete one revolution around the sun, and the planet rotates on its axis once every ten hours and forty-five minutes.

Uranus has a diameter of about 29,300 miles. Its density is twice as great as Saturn's—about 1.56 that of water. The planet's surface gravity is only some 7 percent greater than that of Earth. The sunlight on the planet is so weak that its surface temperature is extremely cold, about minus 300 degrees Fahrenheit.

Greenish in color, Uranus only occasionally shows faint

A comparison of the axial tilt of Uranus to that of five other planets.

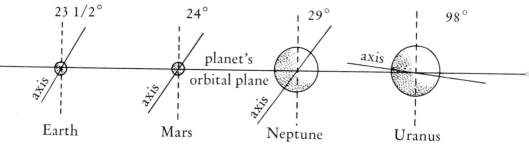

markings like the belts on Jupiter and Saturn. Also like those planets, it has a thick gaseous atmosphere composed of methane and traces of ammonia; hydrogen and helium are also present. Underneath the gaseous atmosphere, astronomers believe there are layers of chemical ice and that the center is a rocky core.

There are two odd facts about Uranus. First, it is the only planet in the solar system to rotate on its axis from east to west; all the others go from west to east. Second, the axis of rotation of Uranus is tilted at a huge angle to its orbit around the sun, greater than that of any other planet to its orbit. Earth's axis is tilted 23½ degrees, Mars's 24, Jupiter's only 3, Saturn's 26½, Neptune's 29. But Uranus is tilted at more than a right angle—98 degrees! Uranus, therefore, goes around the sun lying on its equator, instead

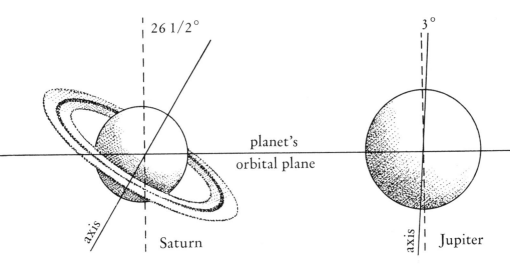

26 1/2°

planet's
orbital plane

axis

Saturn

3°

axis

Jupiter

of orbiting the sun with its axis more or less perpendicular to its orbital plane as the other planets do. In this strange position, the Uranian poles, rather than the equator, alternately face the sun as the planet revolves in its orbit.

This unusual tilt of its axis makes the planet's five known moons all the more interesting, because they revolve very nearly in Uranus's equatorial plane. Thus, the whole Uranian system is one of a planet on its equator rushing through space with its moons whirling about it. When either of Uranus's poles is presented to Earth in a bird's-eye view —as it was in 1945 and will be in 1985—the orbits of the moons will appear circular. But in those years when the Uranian equator is presented to Earth—as was the case in 1966 and will be in 2007—the orbits of the moons will be seen edgewise; that is, the satellites will be seen to pass

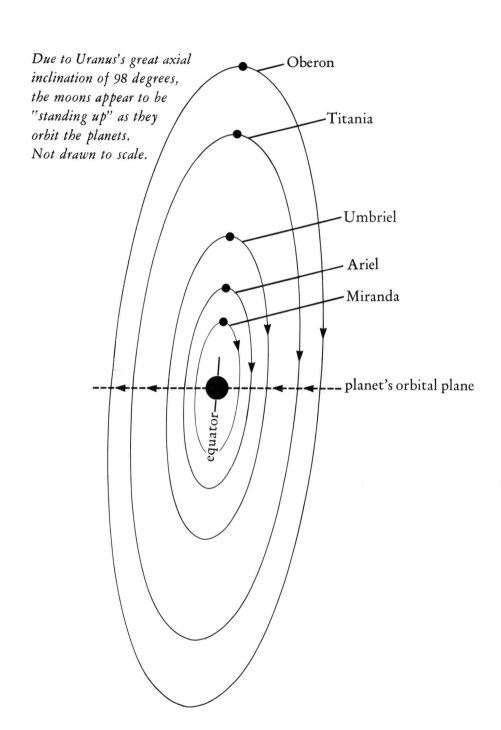

Due to Uranus's great axial inclination of 98 degrees, the moons appear to be "standing up" as they orbit the planets. Not drawn to scale.

Oberon

Titania

Umbriel

Ariel

Miranda

planet's orbital plane

equator

back and forth in a straight line from one side of Uranus to the other. In addition, all of the Uranian satellites orbit their primary very rapidly in the same retrograde motion that Uranus rotates in; that is, from east to west. Though all five satellites are much smaller than our moon, they are denser and none is thought to have an atmosphere. Unlike other moons of the solar system that were given mythological names, those of Uranus were given literary ones.

The Uranian satellites are described below in order of their increasing distance from their primary.

Miranda. The faintest and smallest of the Uranian moons, Miranda was the fifth and last to be found. Kuiper discovered it in 1948. Miranda orbits Uranus at a mean distance of about 80,000 miles, completing one revolution in one day, nine hours, and about fifty minutes. Estimates of its diameter vary from about 100 to 200 miles. Its density is approximated at five times that of water. Nothing definite is known of its physical composition. The moon was named after a character in Shakespeare's *The Tempest.*

Ariel. The English amateur astronomer William Lassell found Ariel in 1851. Estimates of its diameter vary greatly, from 400 to 1500 miles. The satellite revolves around Uranus at a mean distance of about 119,000 miles, completing one full revolution in two Earth days, two hours, and twenty-nine minutes. Its density is thought to be about five times that of water. Ariel's physical composition is unknown.

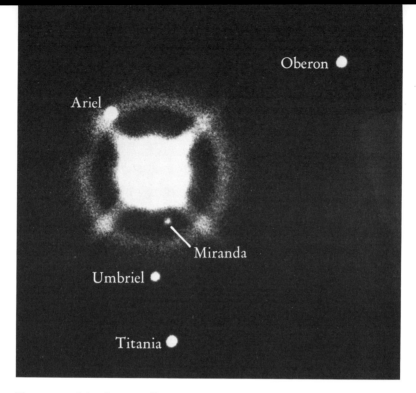

Uranus and its five satellites photographed at the McDonald Observatory, Mount Locke, Texas.

Lassell named Ariel after a sylph (an imaginary being inhabiting the air) in Alexander Pope's *The Rape of the Lock.*

Umbriel. Lassell also discovered this moon at the same time that he found Ariel. Estimates of its diameter run between 300 and 800 miles. Umbriel's period of revolution takes four days, three hours, and twenty-eight minutes. It orbits Uranus at a mean distance of about 166,000 miles. Its density is about four times that of water. The satellite's composition is unknown. Like Ariel, Umbriel was named for a sylph in Pope's *The Rape of the Lock.*

Titania. Possibly the largest of the Uranian moons, Titania was discovered by Herschel in 1787. Estimates of its diameter run as low as 600 miles to as high as 1500 miles. Titania orbits its primary at a mean distance of about 272,000 miles and completes one revolution in eight Earth days, sixteen hours, and fifty-six minutes. The moon is thought to have the highest density of any in its group, at six times that of water. Nothing is known of its composition. Titania was named after the fairy queen in Shakespeare's *A Midsummer Night's Dream.*

Oberon. The outermost of the Uranian satellites, Oberon was discovered by Herschel in the same year he discovered Titania. Its size may be slightly smaller than Titania's, with estimates ranging from 700 to 1500 miles. The satellite orbits Uranus at a mean distance of about 364,000 miles. It completes one revolution of the primary in thirteen days, eleven hours, and seven minutes. Its density is thought to be about five times that of water. Nothing is known definitely of its physical composition. Oberon was named after the fairy king in Shakespeare's *A Midsummer Night's Dream.*

When the Voyager spacecraft, which flew by Jupiter in 1979, reach Uranus in 1986, they may make photographic discoveries of even more moons in orbit around the giant planet.

Neptune
and Its Moons

Far out in the depths of interplanetary space, a thousand million miles beyond the orbit of Uranus, is the last of the giant planets and the eighth from the sun. It is Neptune. If Uranus seems remote and lonely, Neptune is far more so. If an earthman could stand on the Neptunian surface, he would be able to see little of the solar system apart from the shrunken sun. Saturn and Jupiter would be hard to detect. Earth, Mars, Venus, and Mercury would be invisible. Only Uranus and Pluto would be readily seen when sufficiently close in their orbits to Neptune's.

The story of Neptune's discovery is an interesting one. The planet was literally found on paper—by mathematics. After Herschel found Uranus in 1781, other astonomers watching the planet noticed that its orbit wandered slightly from the calculated orbit. Also, up to the year 1822, Uranus seemed to move too rapidly; after that year, it seemed to lag in its orbit. This phenomenon puzzled astronomers, and and it soon became clear that some unknown factor was causing Uranus's strange behavior.

Astronomers had already taken into account the gravitational effects of Jupiter and Saturn on Uranus. But still Uranus wandered more than could be explained. In time, scientists began to think that Uranus's straying from its calculated orbit might be due to the pull of an unknown planet still farther from the sun. Eventually the existence of this new planet was predicted independently by a Frenchman, Urbain J. J. Leverrier, and an Englishman, John C. Adams. Both astronomers came to nearly identical conclusions in their search for the hypothetical planet.

Adams completed his work first, and it was sent to the British astronomer royal, Sir George Airy. Unfortunately for Adams, Airy gave it little attention. Meanwhile, Leverrier finished his calculations and sent them to Johann Enke in Germany in 1846. On Enke's instructions, the German astronomers Johann G. Galle and Heinrich d'Arrest, at the Berlin Observatory, began searching the sky in the position given by Leverrier. Almost at once they identified the body now called Neptune. Because Adam's calculations were finished first but Leverrier's led to the discovery, astronomers give credit to both men.

Physically, Neptune is much like Uranus and is sometimes called "Uranus's twin." Before 1966, it was thought that Neptune was the smaller of the two, at a diameter of 27,700 miles. In that year, however, new calculations placed its diameter at 31,500 miles, establishing Neptune as the larger of the two giant planets. Its density is 1.8 times that of water, almost the same as that of Uranus. Neptune's surface gravity, at 1.5 that of Earth, is also almost the same as that of Uranus.

Both Neptune and Uranus show up as greenish disks in the telescope. The surface temperature of Neptune is lower than Uranus's—about minus 360 degrees Fahrenheit—because it is farther from the sun. But the composition of the two planets is thought to be similar—largely hydrogen and hydrogen compounds, with methane the important constituent of its gaseous atmosphere. Neptune, too, is believed to have a rock core surrounded by layers of chemical ice.

Only in its vastly greater distance from the sun does Neptune cease to be Uranus's twin. Neptune orbits the sun at a mean distance of about 2,793 million miles, which is thirty times the distance of Earth from the sun. The giant planet takes almost 165 Earth years to complete one revolution around the sun. Since its discovery in 1846, it has gone through only about two thirds of a revolution and will not have made a complete one until the year 2011. Yet Neptune is a fast spinner, taking only about fourteen hours to rotate on its axis.

The planet has two known satellites. The closest to Neptune, and by far the largest and brightest, is Triton. It was discovered by Lassell very shortly after Neptune itself was found. Estimates of Triton's diameter range between 2,300 and 3,000 miles, making it larger than our moon.

116

Triton orbits Neptune at a mean distance of about 220,000 miles, which is about the same distance as our moon from Earth. Triton's period of revolution is very short; it fairly streaks around its giant primary in a brief five days and twenty-one hours. Its density is believed to be about five times that of water. The satellite's mass is also high—1.8 times that of our moon. The satellite orbits Neptune in a retrograde direction and is the only large moon in the solar system to have east to west motion. While Triton's orbit is almost circular, it is sharply inclined to Neptune's equator— about 160 degrees.

Because Triton is large and has high density and mass, astronomers think it may have enough gravitational attraction to hold a thin atmosphere. In 1944, Kuiper announced he had found traces of a methane atmosphere by analyzing the reflected sunlight coming from Triton. However, this finding has not been confirmed by other scientists.

One astronomer's calculations indicate that Triton is slowly approaching Neptune and that eventually, in the remote future, the satellite may either collide with its primary or else break up under increasingly severe gravitational strains. Other astronomers have serious doubts about these calculations.

Neptune's second and outermost satellite is Nereid. Too faint to be observed visually through any existing telescope, it was found by Kuiper in 1949 only after it had left its

Neptune and its two satellites. Nereid (upper right arrow), too faint to be observed visually through a telescope, was found in 1949 after its image was left on photographic plates.

image on photographic plates. Nereid's diameter is uncertain, but most estimates place it at about 200 miles. Nothing is known of the little moon's physical makeup.

The remarkable thing about Nereid is its orbit. It is so elliptical that during its period of almost one Earth year, it swings in to Neptune as close as 867,000 miles and then wanders out as far as 6 million miles or more. Its movement around Neptune is from west to east. Some astronomers think that Nereid may be a captured asteroid.

These, then, are the known moons of the sun's family. Are they merely dead and useless worlds of frosty rock,

Orbits of Neptune's two satellites and mean distances from their planet. Note the highly elliptical shape of Nereid's orbit. Distances are approximately to scale.

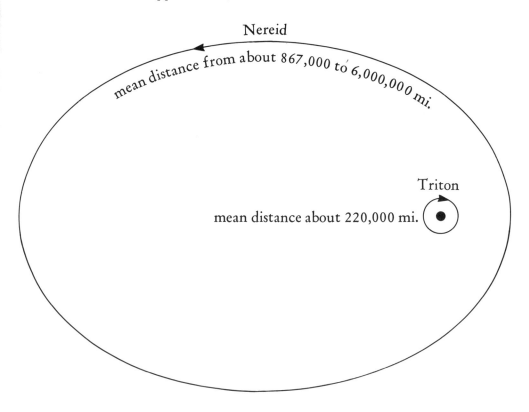

Nereid

mean distance from about 867,000 to 6,000,000 mi.

Triton

mean distance about 220,000 mi.

locked in lonely orbits around their primaries? Of what possible use are these distant satellites that circle planets, which (except for Mars) probably can never be landed on by men?

In this century at least, the moons of the outer giants—Jupiter, Saturn, Uranus, and Neptune—are hopelessly out of range for manned spacecraft from Earth. Only unmanned automatic space probes such as those of the Voyager and Pioneer series, with their cameras electronically poised to send back pictures of "grand tour" expeditions through the solar system, can obtain firsthand information of the outer planets and their moons.

Looking farther ahead, perhaps in the middle decades of the twenty-first century, we can picture the day when manned flights to Jupiter, Saturn, Uranus, and Neptune become possible. Men will land on the satellites of these immense planets and set up lasers, seismometers, cameras, and other equipment in order to study the four largest members of the sun's family. To these astronauts, especially those working on innermost satellites, the planets themselves will appear gigantic and so compellingly dominant in the heavens that men will find it difficult to turn their eyes away from the breathtaking sight.

Perhaps earthmen will choose Io or Callisto from which to study Jupiter; if so, Jupiter will appear to blot out half the sky for much of the time. In the vicinity of Saturn, they may choose Titan or Rhea or Dione. From those moons, astronauts will see the spectacular sight of the rings nearly edgewise, with the innermost satellites rapidly transiting the huge belted disk of Saturn.

Perhaps, to study Uranus, Mission Control will select Titania or Oberon as temporary space stations. Or, in the case of Neptune, astronauts may one day find themselves setting up equipment on that planet's major satellite, Triton. When they pause from their work, they will marvel at their remoteness in the solar system. The sun will be but a brilliant speck in the ebony blackness of interplanetary space. The other major planets, if they can be seen at all, will be hard to detect. Of their home planet Earth, nothing will be seen. And inevitably their eyes will be drawn back to the spectacle of the parent planet brooding in the sky and the bitterly cold gas clouds swirling in its atmosphere.

The existence of these moons may offer man an unparalleled opportunity to win greater knowledge of the solar system in which he lives.

Glossary

asteroid: one of tens of thousands of small planets ranging in size from a few hundred miles to less than a mile in diameter.

atmosphere: the gaseous envelope of a celestial body.

axis: the straight line, real or imaginary, passing through a rotating body about which that body rotates.

celestial body: a general term for all objects that can be observed in the sky beyond Earth's atmosphere; the sun, the moon, the planets and their satellites, comets, stars, etc.

cosmic dust: large clouds of fine particles of matter in interstellar space.

density: the amount of matter in a unit volume of a substance.

disk: the seemingly flat figure of a celestial body as it appears in the sky.

ecliptic: the plane of Earth's orbit around the sun.

ellipse: a plane curve on which the sum of the distances from any point of its circumference to two points within, called the foci, is always the same.

gravitation: the force of attraction that exists among all particles of matter everywhere in the universe.

maria (on the moon): large, dark plains on the surface of the moon; misnamed maria ("seas" in Latin) by Galileo, because they so appeared to him through his telescope.

mascons: large concentrations of massive material in the moon's crust; an acronym coined by scientists from *mass concentrations.*

mass: a measure of the total amount of matter that a (celestial) body contains.

meteoroid: particles of solid matter that exist in, and move through space; meteoroids can be of any size and composition.

moon: in general, a satellite; specifically, the satellite of Earth; *see* natural satellite.

moonquake: a disturbance in the moon's structure resembling an earthquake on Earth.

natural satellite: a celestial body that revolves around one of the planets of the solar system; *see* moon.

nebula: a vast aggregation of matter at stellar distances that shows as a hazy spot or cloud; a gas cloud in space.

occultation: the hiding of one celestial body by another, as when one of the moons of Jupiter passes behind the planet.

orbit: the path of a body that is in revolution about another body, as a natural satellite about its parent body.

period of revolution: in the solar system, the time required for a celestial body, such as a planet, to make one revolution about the sun; also, the time required for a natural satellite to make one revolution around its primary body.

primary: a planet with respect to its natural satellites; the parent body about which its natural satellites revolve.

protoplanet: in theories of the origin of the solar system, a primordial gaseous mass that condenses, cools, and evolves into the present planets; a planet-to-be.

protosun: in theories of the origin of the solar system, a primordial gaseous mass that evolved into the sun; a sun-to-be.

radioactivity: the spontaneous change in the atoms of certain heavy elements, such as radium and uranium, by which they give off radiation and slowly change into different elements.

refracting minerals: minerals, such as thorium, that melt only at very high temperatures.

retrograde motion: a natural satellite that moves from east to west about its primary, instead of from west to east as is normal for most natural satellites in the solar system.

rotational period: the time required for a planet or similar body to turn once on its axis; its "day."

shadow transit: the passage of the shadow of a natural satellite across the disk of its primary.

solar system: the system of the sun and its planets, their satellites, and other objects revolving around the sun.

sun: the star around which Earth and other planets and their natural satellites revolve.

Index
* indicates illustration

126

About the Author

Born in Glens Falls, New York, David C. Knight received his education both in this country and abroad. He earned his B.A. degree at Union College in Schenectady, New York, spent a year at the Sorbonne in Paris, then completed his studies at the Engineering Institute in Philadelphia and at the University of Pennsylvania.

Science has been one of Mr. Knight's major interests. He has worked as an editor and production man with Prentice-Hall and for sixteen years served as senior science editor at Franklin Watts. In addition to the science articles that he has contributed to the *New Book of Knowledge*, Mr. Knight has written many books on various scientific subjects. Particularly well-received among them was *Thirty-Two Moons*, which the *School Library Journal*, in a starred review, called "a unique focus on natural satellites" making it "a good beginner's account of the solar system."

Mr. Knight currently lives in Dobbs Ferry, New York, with his wife and two daughters.